6 BUILDING BLOCKS FOR SUCCESSFUL INNOVATION

T0332048

Innovation is about ideas that make life better. But what does it really take to deliver innovative propositions? And what separates companies that drive their industries forward from those that simply talk the talk?

This book takes you inside the minds of the world's most effective innovators to answer these questions and more. In real stories from industries as diverse as healthcare, finance, technology, and telecommunications, business leaders reveal what it takes to bring new products and services to life. They weigh in on the big debates: how to design an innovative organization of diverse voices, how to protect and grow ideas so they succeed, and how to tune corporate radar to inspiration and turn the signals received into new value.

An essential resource for leaders, aspiring leaders and students of entrepreneurship, business management, HRM, technology and innovation management, and design thinking, the book enables the reader to:

- Hear from leaders with direct responsibility for innovating in a wide range of industries and learn how they do it
- See how to structure for innovation, gain momentum inside an organization, and use ideas to shift companies and industries
- Gain insight into what innovators look for when they sense the environment and learn to avoid common pitfalls and misconceptions that stop great ideas coming to life
- Approach innovation in a more balanced way with the 6 Building Blocks helping you prioritize execution and value delivery from inspiration to implementation

Massimo Garbuio is a Senior Lecturer at the University of Sydney Business School, Australia, where he teaches and researches innovation, design thinking, and strategy.

Moritz Dressel is a consultant in Berlin, Germany. As part of his work with clients large and small, he has developed a reputation for being the go-to guy for companies seeking to become truly data-driven organizations and those that are serious about embarking on meaningful innovation journeys.

6 BUILDING BLOCKS FOR SUCCESSFUL INNOVATION

How Entrepreneurial Leaders Design Innovative Futures

Massimo Garbuio and Moritz Dressel

Routledge
Taylor & Francis Group

LONDON AND NEW YORK

First published 2020
by Routledge
2 Park Square, Milton Park, Abingdon, Oxon OX14 4RN

and by Routledge
52 Vanderbilt Avenue, New York, NY 10017

Routledge is an imprint of the Taylor & Francis Group, an informa business

© 2020 Massimo Garbuio and Moritz Dressel

British Library Cataloguing-in-Publication Data
A catalogue record for this book is available from the British Library

Library of Congress Cataloging-in-Publication Data
A catalog record has been requested for this book

ISBN: 978-0-367-23464-5 (hbk)
ISBN: 978-0-367-23461-4 (pbk)
ISBN: 978-0-429-27994-2 (ebk)

Typeset in Bembo
by Deanta Global Publishing Services, Chennai, India

MIX
Paper from
responsible sources
FSC
www.fsc.org   FSC™ C013985

Printed in the United Kingdom
by Henry Ling Limited

To all aspiring innovators within organizations large and small.

CONTENTS

PART III
Innovation: the future   **155**

ACKNOWLEDGMENTS

We would like to thank first and foremost every single person who we had the pleasure to interview and spend some time with. The book would not exist if it were not for the very exciting stories and journeys you have been willing to share with the rest of the world. We are convinced that your wealth of experience across industries and countries, shared in this book, will make a tremendous difference to many aspiring innovators.

We would also like to thank the people who helped us review the questions originally drafted for our interviews. You helped us to make them crisper and more focused, enabling us to distill inspiring lessons from our interviewees. Several of our interviewees said: umm, I like these questions, they make me take some time, sit down, and think about my own personal view on innovation and articulate it. Thank you! Thanks to Josh Mahaney from Orlando Magic, John Corleto from Future Brands, Carlos Vazquez, PhD student at the University of Sydney Business School and ex-Global Innovation Delivery Manager at Pernod Ricard Winemakers, and Paul Slezak from RecruitLoop, who was so passionate about the project and ultimately ended up as interviewee, too. John Corleto, you have been part of this book in so many iterations that you do deserve the biggest THANK YOU!

Thank you, Bastian Schuetz and Francesca Appiani, for getting us access to some amazing individuals, Mark and Carlo! Lucy McClune, Sophie Peoples, and Rebecca Marsh from Routledge as well as Fiona Crawford, Carolin Window, and Letitia Prince were of great help in the publishing and editing process.

Thank you, Kelli Buchholz, for making your internship a book internship! Thank you, Philipp Fuhrig, Samuel Jackson, Suthida Mattayasuwan, Steffen Meilsoe, Drew Tanner, Giulia Teso, and Trevor Watson, for providing invaluable feedback on various manuscript drafts. Drew made us think harder about some critical points. Your views complemented each other and really pushed us to think harder about some aspects of the book and how to better convey the messages. Some of the work included in the book emerged while Massimo was in Jackson Hole – thank you Berne and Jeffrey for the most special time in such an inspiring place.

Last but not least, we would like to thank those who have (involuntarily) been closest to this project. Thank you to Wesley and Bella, Melanie and Noah, and all our families and friends for their patience and support while we have been on this exciting journey.

ABOUT THE AUTHORS

Massimo Garbuio is a Senior Lecturer in Entrepreneurship at the University of Sydney Business School, Australia. Working at the intersection of design thinking and strategy, Massimo's research explores how master strategists think about innovation and disruption, allocate resources, and make decisions. Collaborative research projects include global studies with the *McKinsey Quarterly* and the Australian Association of Private Equity and Venture Capital. Massimo actively participates in shaping public opinion on innovation, writing and speaking for the *Australian Financial Review*, SBS, and *The Conversation*. He has published in global academic journals, including the *California Management Review*, *Design Studies*, *The Academy of Management Learning and Education*, *Long Range Planning*, and *Journal of Management*. He is a member of the Strategic Management Society, the Design Research Society, and the Academy of Management as well as being on the Editorial Board for the *Journal of Management*. He is a co-author of the book *Healthcare Entrepreneurship*, published by Routledge.

Moritz Dressel is an ex-Deloitte management consultant with deep expertise in enabling strategic business transformations across various industries, including manufacturing, financial services, life sciences, consumer business, energy, and utilities. As part of his work with clients large and small, he has developed a reputation for being the go-to guy for companies seeking to become truly data-driven organizations and those that are serious about embarking on meaningful innovation journeys.

Moritz is also the author of the number-one survival guide for consulting career starters, *The Aspiring Advisor – Strategies & Tools for a Successful Consulting Career*, and *Got the Job… Now What? How to Master the Corporate Game from Day 1.*

PART I

Innovation: getting started

1

INTRODUCTION

Wherever you look, there is change. But not change of the evolutionary type. We are talking about change that is fundamentally shifting how the global ecosystem works. Exponential growth of new technologies, as well as the near dissolution of time and space, has created a competitive environment unlike any other. Disruption through innovation is the name of the game.

And given the choice between being *disrupted* and being *disrupting*, most would opt for the latter. A potential death threat constantly in sight, the pursuit of innovation has become not just a wise business strategy but a necessity for organizations large and small. For leaders everywhere the catchphrase is adapt or die.

But when we talk about innovation, what do we really mean? In your pursuit of innovation, where do you start? How do you "do" innovation?

There is no shortage of concepts. Practitioners and scholars alike are designing frameworks, processes, and theories to make companies more innovative, to make sense of innovation ecosystems, to get people to work together in new ways, and to "do" innovation. If you are in business, you have probably come across terms like disruptive innovation or radical innovation. You might have firsthand experience in design thinking or human-centered design. Lean start-ups and agile might be bandied around at your organization. No longer the province of the young and entrepreneurial, innovation has gone mainstream, and both practice and academia promise ways to deliver innovation across your company. Innovation approaches are myriad and range from incubators and accelerators to hackathons and TV shows like *Shark Tank* that are aimed at the broader public. The chapters and interviews in this book will help you to understand both what innovation is and how it is done; further suggestions appear in "Resources" in Part 3.

In our experience, the variety of different yet similar approaches for developing something new is confusing. Whenever we engage with clients, they ask, "What is everyone else doing in terms of innovation? How did they start their journey? How did they make it a company-wide thing? What should we focus on and how?"

There is a wealth of academic research on innovation, but it doesn't have all the answers. Research, by its very nature, cannot always be up to date with what's going on in the real world. While research looks retrospectively at what has happened, disruption from clever start-ups is challenging industries such as banking, insurance, and retail as well as real estate, healthcare, and beyond. Where both research and practice agree is that innovation is no longer an option, it is a necessity. To stay relevant a company must innovate. And to innovate, you need to find a novel solution to an existing problem or create a vision for a bright new future.

If you're reading this book, it's likely that you want to know how to "do innovation." How do you avoid the mistakes other innovators have already made? How do you learn from their experience? Should you hire a consulting or design firm to help you jump-start your innovation journey? Or do you try to go it alone in implementing the idea you read in a business magazine you picked up at the airport?

6 Building Blocks for Successful Innovation: How Entrepreneurial Leaders Design Innovative Futures provides the answers.

6 Building Blocks for Successful Innovation is unique in its combining of firsthand innovation experience from various fields with a strong scientific foundation. Armed with years of academic research and consulting experience, we make our case for how to be more innovative. Moreover, we illustrate this with the experience of successful leaders who have championed innovation in their fields, and we tell you what worked and what didn't work in their innovation journeys (see Part 2).

The choice of some interviewees may seem obvious, while others are perhaps less well-known advocates of innovation. However, all of those interviewed for this book are uniquely qualified to contribute. Whether it is the entrepreneur who has been building and scaling his venture from the ground up or the corporate veteran who has continuously kept her organization (and, in fact, the industry) at the forefront by repeated paradigm-shifting innovation, each one has provided his or her candid view on the keys to innovating successfully and what pitfalls to avoid.

While you might think you have a good idea about what innovation is and what it looks like, when you ask a range of people, a plethora of views emerge. The same can be said for our interview partners. Despite answering the same set of questions, their responses could not have been more varied and intriguing. Their responses suggest that innovation is new products, services, and business models. That *sometimes* it is driven by technology. That it's about business processes – internal and external. That it's all of these things and more.

Who should read this book?

We have aimed this book at an audience of entrepreneurial and innovative people within established companies. We attempt to shed light on the questions we have been asked over the years by those starting an innovation journey within their organization. We also try to provide answers to questions raised by those who have started an innovation journey but have hit a plateau or roadblock.

If you are a student of innovation, *6 Building Blocks for Successful Innovation* will bring to life many of the theories and frameworks you hear about in the classroom, complementing the cases that you discuss in class with experiences from other contexts. And you will encounter very different perspectives, because our synthesis of research and practice acknowledges the drawbacks of theories and frameworks in the real world.

Everybody starting out on an innovation journey will find something of interest in these pages. Likewise, seniority is no precondition to benefiting from this book. It may be easier to set a baseline for your innovation journey if you have autonomy. But as you will learn from the interviews, hierarchical levels (or age, for that matter) are largely irrelevant when it comes to making an impact through innovation. Young upstarts may have to work harder to have their ideas accepted. But equipped with the lessons from the innovators in this book, even the most junior prospective innovator should be well positioned to cause disruption. Those more senior, to which new ideas are presented, will be empowered to provide guidance to their colleagues. Through the lessons of amazing innovators – those actually engaging in innovation – we want you to unlock your individual innovative capability and help you empower the people around you to do the same.

How to read this book

We suggest you start reading with Chapter 2, "Innovation: A Definition," to gain a useful overview, and then look at Chapters 3–5. This should give you the big picture. Then read the interviews. They don't have to be read in order, as each has a unique flavor while also confirming and complementing each other.

Once you've read through the interviews, we recommend you return to Chapters 3–5 to reflect on what it means for your own journey. Where are you now? What should be next? What is standing in the way of where you want to be? What fixes can you implement today in your company? Sometimes even a small change in attitude or mindset can have a substantial impact on your company's innovation potential and, eventually, bottom line. This book aims to guide you to make the *best* choices. Ultimately, your first choice should be to take action.

In order to support you on your innovation journey, we have included a selection of tools and concepts from the world of innovation in "Resources" in Part 3. There is no shortage of concepts – and that is precisely why it's easy to lose your way on the road to innovation. Informed by both the interviews and our academic research, we hope this road map to innovation will make the journey smooth and rapid.

2

INNOVATION

A Definition

Imagine the following scenario: you have been asked to drive the innovation agenda within your company. This is the opportunity you have always wanted. But you also have a great idea for a start-up. What should you do – the opportunity your company is offering will give you visibility with the C-suite and put the company on an unprecedented transformation path, but you are also excited about branching out on your own. Should you take a huge risk and start something new that will see you living like a student for the next five years until you turn a profit? Or should you create something amazing within your current company?

While you are tempted by creating your own start-up, you are also excited that you have finally been recognized as an innovator and asked to build and lead an innovation team. You decide to take this opportunity within your organization because it allows you to be creative, to think outside the box, and to empower other people to do fun stuff that will make an impact in the organization and possibly beyond.

Then people start asking you: what is your agenda? How are you going to go about it? Do we need innovation? Aren't we the market leader already? Someone else might say, we are already innovative, why do we need some new program? Others may discourage you by saying the company will never be innovative because it has too much bureaucracy or an inhibiting culture. And how do you get the buy-in of all decision makers? And what is innovation anyway? It all seems a lot harder than you thought it would be.

In *6 Building Blocks for Successful Innovation*, we don't worry about the question of whether we need innovation in the first place. Nor do we provide all possible arguments to counter potential resistance. But we do provide you with nuggets of wisdom and very practical learnings from innovators around the globe that will inspire and guide you along your innovation journey.

Before we get into it, let's answer one more question though, perhaps the first question you will be asked. What is innovation, anyway?

In talking about innovation, different people mean different things. We all have an idea. You might think that the first iPhone was an innovation. Others might think that Coco Chanel was a true innovator. Innovation is, perhaps, one of the most misinterpreted terms. Then there are all the subsets of innovation such as sustaining innovation, radical innovation, incremental innovation, or even disruptive innovation. What do these all mean?

We do not distinguish between innovating products, services, or business models. Similarly, we don't focus on technology-driven innovation, user-driven innovation, or the innovation of meaning.[1] Ultimately, it is really just about "innovation."

To make clear what we mean by just "innovation," we refer to a definition we have arrived at based on a systematic review of a multidisciplinary set of studies which, over the years, has attracted more than 1,000 citations and has therefore become one of the most often cited articles in a prestigious journal on innovation. Our objective is to provide a comprehensive view of organizational innovation, including definitions from the different disciplinary literatures of economics, innovation and entrepreneurship, business and management, and technology, science, and engineering. The general and integrative definition of organizational "innovation" that encompasses the different perspectives is as follows:[2]

> Innovation is the multistage process whereby organizations transform ideas into new/improved products, services, or processes, in order to advance, compete, and differentiate themselves successfully in their marketplace.

We like this definition because it starts to give us a sense of what innovation is. First, it is not necessarily something that happens in a brainstorming session. It takes time to come up with an innovative idea. It can be a solo process rather than a team effort. Even a solo process may stem from the formation of an idea over a longer period of time, drawing on inspiration from disparate sources, studies, travel, and discussions with experts and non-experts. It means that an idea is conceptualized by one individual rather than a team. And even if an idea is conceptualized in an instant, it is still the result of incubation over a long period.

Second, it starts with raw materials, namely, ideas. Our role as innovators is to collect them and transform them into something else.

Third, it's about improvement, broadly speaking, of products, services, or processes, and so incorporates the concept of business models.

Fourth, the outcome is about some type of advancement, competition, and differentiation in the marketplace. It should ultimately have a meaningful impact on the bottom line.[3]

The purpose of the definition above is to lay the foundation for what comes next. Keep it in mind as you read on, because it provides a practical and flexible interpretation of innovation. We now invite you to dive into the minds of our innovators to learn how they view innovation and how to go about it.

Notes

1 We will discuss these concepts and approaches in the various interviews.
2 Baregheh, A., Rowley, J., & Sambrook, S. (2009). Towards a multidisciplinary definition of innovation. *Management Decision, 47*(8), 1323–1339.
3 Another definition is presented by IDEO, perhaps the most well-known innovation and design consulting firm, which was established in 1991 in California. According to them, innovation is what satisfies three conditions: desirability, viability, and feasibility. In other words, it has to create value for the user and make them want your product or service. It has to create a viable business that will make a profit, and it has to be feasible, that is, it can be achieved in the foreseeable future. This has become part of the common language of any innovator who starts from the user and his or her pain points to design new solutions and business models.

3

6 BUILDING BLOCKS FOR INNOVATION

An overview

All you need to know to start and speed up an innovation journey.

If you follow a strict innovation process, you may end up changing it every time the latest management trend takes hold. We give you 6 Building Blocks that have stood the test of time. They are the result of the years of experience of the innovators we interviewed and act as catalysts for innovation. They have been tested in different industries, in different parts of the world, by people with very different functional backgrounds and at different stages in their careers. They can be applied to any innovation context.

Innovation process: yes, but...

The idea of a magic formula, a straightforward equation in which "x + y = innovation," is attractive. We often think about innovation as a process comprised of a finite number of steps that, if followed one by one, will inevitably lead to the "Aha!" moment. It will seem like you have reached the end of your innovation journey and you can sit back and reap the rewards. A process is also attractive for educators, as its linear nature suggests you can teach the various steps and provides the illusion that some magic will happen at the end.

Having a process is great for ensuring consistency in output over time, across teams, and even across countries. The quality of the Coca-Cola you drink in the US is the same as the one you drink in Germany or Australia. The quality of the customer service at an Apple Store is consistent around the world. Processes work for organizations, whether it is the idea of following strict routines for daily procedures or sticking to company guidelines when pursuing new projects. The idea behind them is simple: to mitigate risks.[1]

But does this work for innovation? Do you follow a strict process, perhaps detailed in a thick manual, and come up with innovative ideas? Not quite.

The problem is that risks need to be taken from time to time. A strict process restricts the whole concept behind innovation. The best ideas come from creative and free-flowing minds, not from policies that do not just avoid risk but that also restrict the ability to think freely.

The use of strict processes and planning to nurture innovation used to be the norm. Capturing opportunities was shaped by planning through meticulous business-plan development and systematic searches.[2] In fact, that is still the case today. As we know from our consulting work, many large corporations (some of which represent very famous brands) continue to operate as if there has been no move toward digital since the late 1980s. However, the highly dynamic business environment we live in today is shaped by rapid changes in technology. This requires the ability to sense and digest a large amount of information, to create meaningful hypotheses about the future, and to learn to quickly grasp opportunities. In order to stay relevant, companies must foster innovation by encouraging a testing mindset and accepting occasional failure rather than encouraging process compliance.

When individuals follow strict processes, their minds are directed toward one specific end goal rather than being open to alternative, creative ideas that may lead in a whole new direction. In design and creativity, it is understood that a rigid process does not work, as it may lead to fixation, "a blind, and sometimes counterproductive adherence to a limited set of ideas in the design process."[3] So while there are benefits to innovation processes, they also carve out a narrow path that doesn't allow for exploring unchartered territory.

At this point, we want to give you a preview of an important insight from our interviews: If you need to latch onto something, some basic frameworks are more useful than others. There are some frameworks or even theories that are so simple that they do not need much interpretation. These are often also the ones that withstand the test of time. They are broad enough to allow some flexibility in thinking and adaptation over time. Think about the IDEO diagram on Design Driven Innovation or the Three Horizon Model.[4] (To find out more about these, see "Resources" in Part 3.)

Against that background, we have distilled our findings and identified what we call the 6 Building Blocks for Innovation. You can have agile, scenario planning, design thinking, and all of that – but at the end of the day, chasing the next trend is not going to help you. A lot of it is just noise, the perennial quest of scholars and practitioners to make their own stamp rather than make a meaningful difference.[5]

The 6 Building Blocks

Before we go into more detail in the following two chapters, we will briefly introduce the blocks. We classify them into two parts: the "Core" and the "Frontier." Each consists of important principles that are fundamental in starting and speeding up your innovation journey.

6 BUILDING BLOCKS

FOR LEADING SUCCESSFUL INNOVATION

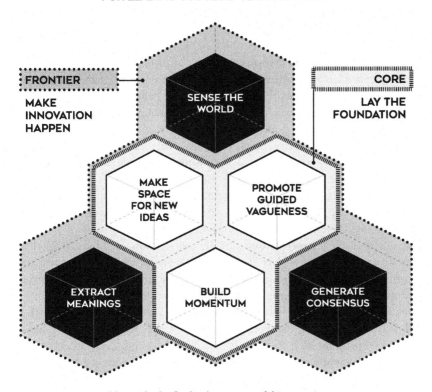

FIGURE 3.1   6 Building Blocks for leading successful innovation

The **Core** is comprised of three blocks defining and establishing the foundations of innovative endeavors. These foundations must be "right" from the start because they will affect everything that is built upon them in the innovation process. If the Core is not strong, the rest of the framework will not withstand the external challenges of innovation.

The first block within the Core is **Make Space for New Ideas**. This is where you lay the critical foundations of the new innovation team and establish how this team relates to the rest of the organization and engages with ideas. This is where you set the ground rules for the organization. A key principle here is that you don't need to transform every single person in the organization into an innovation machine. Not everyone needs to be engaged in innovation, but everyone should appreciate that innovation needs to be part of the organization's DNA.

The second block is **Promote Guided Vagueness**. Innovators experiment all the time but usually within boundaries. Hence, typical KPIs are rarely effective, and costs and revenue budgets just don't work for innovation. Some people even say you should have a virtual P&L for innovation. But everyone agrees that innovation is about learning and being free to explore a new world, not delivering against strictly predefined outcomes. It is more beneficial to guide rather than manage an innovation process. By leaving room for vagueness as well as unpredictability, you will develop a more successful and innovative outcome instead of reaching a dead end.

The third block is **Build Momentum**. As an innovation team, you can't wait for layers within your organization to give you permission and constantly approve your progress. You can't even wait for a big budget to be approved and the buy-in from many departments, all with their own goals (whether justified or otherwise) and their own political agendas. You need to be quick to keep up with the fast-paced world outside your company, where start-ups in garages are changing the way industries operate, and consumers have access to a vast range of products, services, and brands in a globalized environment.

These three blocks (ideally) are at the center of your innovation journey if you are to set yourself up for success. But to substantially increase your chances for success, the Core building blocks of innovation are not sufficient.

This is where the **Frontier** comes in. It, too, consists of three blocks that interact with internal stakeholders (think senior leadership) as well as the broader environment. The actions within these blocks cannot be completed without a boost from the respective internal blocks surrounding the Core.

Block four, essentially the first block within the Frontier, is called **Sense the World**. It is about **sensing** the world around you, collecting data, or more specifically, generating the *right* data (about trends, technologies, etc.) to empower you to think differently about innovation. Innovation happens at intersections between different domains. So you should pay more attention to domains other than your own customers and competitors here. Good data will allow you to come up with good options. Sensing mechanisms follow the Make Space for New Ideas block established in the Core. Without a solid foundation for the organization in the Core, it may be difficult to explore the external environment in a useful way.[6]

The fifth block, **Extract Meanings**, is where you transition from data to insights, often taking shape as hypotheses about a new future. It's about the value that you create for an existing or a new customer. This is determined by the data you have, but it's also empowered by the freedom that you have, thanks to the openness to vagueness that has been made explicit in your organization in the Core. As a result of eliminating the old, restrictive KPI system, you can push the boundaries and take unexpected paths by following business models and new visions about the future that will create meaning.

Finally, there is the block called **Generate Consensus**. This is where you generate ideas and sell them to relevant stakeholders. At this point, establishing relationships with internal stakeholders is key. You can't tell them, "I have this great idea" and expect them to jump on-board. You can't bring everyone together in a room, from the engineers to the finance people, and expect them to trust your idea. You need to get everyone to join you on the journey by telling powerful, meaningful stories. And you need to do this both speedily and step by step. If you wait too long to establish these relationships, you may miss out on the benefits the internal stakeholders can provide throughout your innovation journey. But if you rush them, you risk alienating them.

This brief summary of the 6 Building Blocks will now be expanded on in the next two chapters. Take a deep breath and dive in.

Notes

1 Total quality management is indeed a way to pursue efficacity improvements, eliminate waste, and achieve sustainable development. It is not a process for innovation.

2 There has been significant debate in entrepreneurship research about how to teach entrepreneurship and, more specifically, whether opportunities for new ventures can be discovered through a planning process, or they emerge as the result of an enactment process. Research has now moved beyond this to talk about ideas and opportunities. Alvarez, S. A., & Barney, J. B. (2010). Entrepreneurship and epistemology: The philosophical underpinnings of the study of entrepreneurial opportunities. *Academy of Management Annals*, 4(1), 557–583.

3 See Garbuio, M., Dong, A., Lin, N., Tschang, T., & Lovallo, D. (2018). Demystifying the genius of entrepreneurship: How design cognition can help create the next generation of entrepreneurs. *Academy of Management Learning & Education*, 17(1), 41–61.

4 See Baghai, M., Coley, S., & White, D. (2000). *The Alchemy of Growth*. Reading, MA: Basic Books. For an updated and similar approach, see also, Nagji, B., & Tuff, G. (2012). Managing your innovation portfolio: People throughout your organization are energetically pursuing the new. But does all that activity add up to a strategy? *Harvard Business Review*, 66–73.

5 Roberto Verganti argues that the world is awash with ideas and information and we need the time to reflect and generate insights. See Verganti, R. (2017). *Overcrowded: Designing Meaningful Products in a World Awash with Ideas*: MIT Press. This reminds us of Warren Buffett and his idea that we are given a card and we can punch 20 holes in our lifetime, 20 investment decisions that will really make a difference. See Schroeder, A. (2008). *The Snowball: Warren Buffett and the Business of Life*. London, UK: Bloomsbury.

6 In innovation, as in entrepreneurship, the ecosystem around an innovator and a company may have a tremendous impact on what is really possible. And this is set by the funding that a state has made available to entrepreneurs and companies alike. In an insightful book, Mariana Mazzucato discusses how public investments in innovation have shaped the future of many start-ups that in the end have been acquired by companies that we consider innovative, including but not limited to Apple. This should make you reflect on to what extent your and your company's efforts are aligned to your state's investments. Mazzucato, M. (2013). *The Entrepreneurial State: Debunking the Public vs. Private Myth in Risk and Innovation*. London, UK: Anthem.

4

BUILDING BLOCKS FOR INNOVATION

The Core

The innovation journey starts from "the Core." We focus on the key things that must be done to create a fertile environment for ideas. What follows is an in-depth discussion of each block within the Core, typically supported by a handful of key ideas, which we refer to as principles. By making explicit reference to the interviews with the innovation leaders, you will gain practical insights and see the concepts come to life.

Block 1: make space for new ideas

- Principle 1: focus your innovation efforts by including those who are ready to step up
- Principle 2: create space for the people working on innovation
- Principle 3: build trust among the people involved in innovation through organizational design

When you hear the word innovation, what happens? Do you get excited? Given you have picked up this book and read thus far, you probably think of yourself as a "shaper" rather than a "consumer" of the future. So when it comes to innovation, you may be keen to get into the swing of things yourself and enjoy creative thought and execution. Perhaps this comes with a desire for freedom and autonomy. But within your current environment the challenge seems enormous. You start thinking: "I have to evangelize the entire organization. Everyone has to know that we are a little bit different, and everyone has to be innovative and contribute new ideas." Of course, you think about some big names and how innovative they were, and you think that everyone should be passionate about it, run innovation projects, participate in idea contests, and so on. And if it was solely up to you, new ways of working would be adopted, and everyone would be trained in "design thinking" and start talking about "agile" and "lean." How else can your company get ahead?

Stop! There are other, smarter ways. You don't need a big bang to initiate innovative action. Going all-in against all the odds is a sure recipe for disaster.

The reality is that most of the organization's revenue *today* does not come from new products and services. It most probably comes from the same old nuts and bolts the company has worked with for a long time. The company's main business is still products that have been tested and tweaked over time and that are perfectly fine for today's market.

What does that mean for innovation, and, more specifically, for kick-starting an innovation journey through designing the new organization?

The first key idea here – the **first principle** – is that you should **focus your innovation efforts by including those who are ready to step up**. There is no natural law requiring you to change the company culture in order to become a more innovative company. In other words, you don't need to make everyone innovative in the same way. You don't need to run extensive innovation workshops nor have everyone on board. You need a group of people, however small, provided there is a good mix, that focuses on innovation. The rest of the organization can have a taste of it, but they don't need much more than that.[1]

Our interview with **Tim Romero**, who is Chief Technology Officer within the Business Innovation Task Force of Tokyo Electric Power Company (TEPCO), a Japanese electric utility holding company, and the host of the Disrupting Japan Podcast, argues that you do not need to buy into all the hype about changing entire corporate cultures to be more innovative (as some consultants may have you believe). He tells the story of the San Francisco Bay Area, considered the most innovative place on the planet. As he points out, only 0.5% of the population is doing anything that's innovative. The rest are going about daily life, doing jobs that keep society running, like teaching and nursing. These jobs are as important as innovators – without them society cannot function.

So how should innovation be approached – in particular, what should executives and politicians do to support the bubbling up of innovative ideas.[2] The answer – nothing new! Consider one of the most famous frameworks – the Three Horizons of Growth – which was published in 2000.[3] It is mentioned by two of our interviewees, Mark Nierwetberg and Stefan Vlachos, and is still very popular among consultants. In a nutshell, the framework is based on the assumption that working at improving today's core business is not enough to stay competitive in the long term. Parts of the organization should be devoted to taking ideas that have worked in a pilot or somewhere else in the world and growing them into new core businesses. But the rest of the organization should just focus on tinkering and running experiments. Importantly, those working on any one of those three activities – ideally, three different types of people – should be rewarded according to metrics that make sense for these objectives. Performance metrics should not be applied across the board but tailored appropriately. So whoever is working in the core business should keep working in the core business and delivering revenue growth and cost-efficiency. They need to stay close to the customers and be aware of and open to issues and opportunities, yet they should not have responsibility for innovation, especially not a blue-sky type of innovation. Indeed, the closer you are to the customer, the more focused on the details rather than the big picture and future trends you should be.

The **second principle** (and a consequence of the previous one) is that you need to **create space for the people working on innovation**. At times, you might have to separate the people working on innovation from the rest of the company.[4]

Stefan Vlachos, the Head of the Center for Innovation at the Karolinska University Hospital, comments on this when he describes how hospitals have kept their innovators close to their patients, with the rest of the employees. However, as new methods are considered for the future structure of the hospital, a separate space may be more appropriate. In his day-to-day life, Vlachos and his team are working hard to find effective ways to incubate or accelerate a more innovation-oriented way of thinking into a dedicated part of the hospital. He argues that while establishing a separate innovation team in hospitals may be more difficult to accomplish, he's convinced that it's a good idea.

Similarly, **Mark Nierwetberg**, the Senior Vice President for Transformation Office Technology & Innovation at Deutsche Telekom, states that to create innovative thinking in your company, you need to provide appropriate space. If executives or managers consider "playing around" a waste of time, then innovation will never flourish. What is required instead is a certain degree of freedom. Innovators need to be enabled to express and develop their ideas without restriction. According to Nierwetberg, this should indeed apply to anyone, both established innovators and innovators-to-be. Based on his experience, anyone in the workplace can develop an innovative idea if given the opportunity.

Melissa Widner, a General Partner at NAB ventures (NAB, one of the largest financial institutions in Australia), mostly shares the views of Vlachos and Nierwetberg. She reflects on how NAB Labs provides a way for innovators to remove themselves from their company to focus solely on their innovative process. She discusses how the Labs were started as an innovation hub to develop and test new products. Working outside of the bank's main business, and partnering with external companies, makes it easier to experiment and allows for the lessons that come with failure.

In a similar vein, **Peter Löfgren**, Managing Director of SynerLeap, industrial giant ABB's innovation growth hub, underscores the importance of becoming an active participant in an innovation ecosystem. That's what Löfgren and his team set out to accomplish with SynerLeap. It doesn't matter who the individual actors are – start-up, government, company – what matters is the ecosystem. Operating alone, outside of the ecosystem is not conducive to effective innovation.

Creating some separate space for members of an organization to tinker with innovative ideas is one thing. Going beyond and opening up to external parties, like both NAB and ABB are doing, is another. Most certainly, opening up – if done right – is not easy for most corporations. Letting go, and potentially losing the right to be in charge of everything that happens within one's ecosystem, can be a stretch for some corporate settings. Löfgren acknowledges that it's difficult to let go of control and to expose oneself to risk. But he sees that trying to keep control is short-sighted because it stifles activity in the ecosystem, which actually increases risk. He argues that if you try to minimize risk you force the ecosystem to stand still, which actually ends up increasing risk. This is because standing still is the slow path to failure. By giving innovators a safe place with room for failure, you unlock growth and potential innovative success.

Note that internal R&D Labs (see next chapter) and Innovation Centers or Labs are very different things. The former may work well, as they are geared towards hardcore innovation. The latter have recently become the subject of discussion in both consulting and academia.[5] Whether inside or outside an organization, they are often created to give innovation an almost religious status, that sees it excluded – and protected – from the rest of the organization. In a very insightful conversation with Sandra Peters (and in the work of Ella Hafermalz in her PhD thesis),[6] Dirk Hovorka illustrates the findings of their study. He outlines that at the beginning, innovation ideas often need to be protected from the burden of commercialization. However, this also positions innovation as weak and defenseless, not as a serious part of the organization.[7] As Professor Hovorka says,

> Perhaps more fundamentally, this points to the need to question our assumptions about how innovation happens. We tend to assume innovation is basically a linear process, the outcome of predictable, manageable stages, when in practice substantive innovations – think iPods or Uber – have relied on making disparate connections between ideas, products and services.[8]

We won't lie to you: there is no right or wrong answer in terms of whether to keep those involved in innovation close to the organization or more detached. We recommend you do two things: read what the leaders share in their interviews and dig a little deeper. Perhaps check on your competition and beyond in terms of what others are doing and why.[9] Then ask yourself:

1. Will the rest of the organization kill or boycott any innovation attempt, because of, for example, strong personalities or politics? If so, you need to protect the innovation team. This is crucial when starting out. Once the team has gained some traction and credibility, you can start considering ways to engage other parts of the organization. But do this with caution.
2. Does the rest of the organization need to be exposed to what's happening in the innovation area, perhaps because they are way behind the competition? Do they understand that the threat to survival is real? If so, find ways to provide exposure and take others along on the journey by offering them the opportunity to observe.

3. If you want to bring in start-ups, what is the desired impact? Are you looking for financial benefits, or do you want to learn from them and spread
   some of the entrepreneurial culture across the rest of the organization? And
   to what extent can you grant access to internal resources for external start-
   ups, marketing, logistics, engineering, and so on?

Fundamentally, clarify your objectives for engaging in an innovation journey
(which should almost never be just a marketing thing) and then consider where
to place innovation, physically.

The **third** and final principle of the first block is the importance of the organizational design to **build trust among the people involved in innovation**.
Trust is crucial to sharing ideas (regardless of whether fully thought through or
otherwise). It allows people to express themselves without being judged and to
ultimately develop more daring concepts.

Victoria Vallströ̈m (Bastide), the CFO at Lifesum, underscores the importance of establishing team trust and believes that individuals must take the risk of
trusting each member of the team to create what she calls psychological safety.
After all, no one will dare to experiment and go out on a limb if they think they
will be punished. According to her, although trusting someone immediately
after establishing a team may seem risky, it is ultimately the most effective way to
establish a sense of psychological safety throughout the remainder of the group
work.[10]

In our interview with **Peter Löfgren**, we also discussed the importance of
instilling trust among team members, especially if this involves people from
both inside and outside the organization. According to him, it is important to
allow for serendipity by enabling informal conversations over coffee and other
semi-social interactions. He encourages people to talk about anything that is
nonconfidential in order to build trust and gain understanding of their inten-
tion to invest in the relationship – are they serious about changing the future?
Likewise, if innovation is about engaging with start-ups, then a relationship of
trust needs to be established. The start-up needs to know that the corporation
is not seeking to steal ideas or solutions but wants to work together to develop
and acquire, for example, faster and newer technology. It won't happen overnight – it takes time and a commitment to collaboration. But the rewards can
be invaluable.

In a similar vein, **Paul Slezak,** the CEO of RecruitLoop, goes on to call on
team leaders to give people the opportunity to speak up and make suggestions.
These suggestions may be made confidentially in relation to their own job, or
in relation to what they are doing in the business, or about the bigger picture of
the direction of the business. Regardless of how valuable the suggestion may be,
people need to know that they are heard. Whether the team leader is going to
take action or otherwise, he or she should be open about it. If the team leader
is going to act on the suggestion, then credit has to be given. Credit inspires
other people in the organization to come to their team leaders with smart ideas.

Importantly, this really brings out those people who are shy, those who may be thinking more deeply rather than talking, those who have reflected more thoroughly on issues facing customers or faced by the company. Because they may not feel comfortable speaking up when an innovative idea comes to mind, these ideas may be left unspoken if action is not taken; however, if these individuals and other team members recognize the importance of their position on the team and feel comfortable in a team setting, they will be more likely to trust their fellow team members, leading to more collaboration and willingness to make important contributions that benefit the team.

Block 2: promote guided vagueness

- Principle 1: establish guidance while keeping some lack of structure
- Principle 2: help people (who may collaborate anyway) collaborate prolifically
- Principle 3: have your focus firmly set on objectives and avoid rigid KPIs

Now that we have clarified who the innovators are and where they should be placed (that is, how close to the rest of the company they should be), we will talk about accountability and rewards. As you will see, innovators have to be handled differently, and even highly standardized corporate processes like budget allocation should follow different rules from the rest of the company.

As an innovator, what do you need to do? Fundamentally, you need to take risks. You need to experiment with things that don't exist yet. You need to try things out. Otherwise, true discovery cannot take place. If people are rewarded for increasing revenues or cutting costs, you are not likely to reap a whole lot of innovation. Instead, learning – incremental, quick learning – should be encouraged. And you need to do that as a team.

Consider the story of a CEO of a multinational hotel chain and the way he organizes his one-on-one meetings with national CEOs. In these meetings, he asks them to tell him six things. He wants to hear two things that went well in the previous period, two things that he should know, and two things that went not so well. Why? Because he wants them to try things out and be comfortable with risk taking and potential failure. No one is punished for taking risks. If risks aren't taken, the company's growth opportunities are stifled.

The **first principle** is that setting some basic, broad rules rather than adopting a specific process and changing it frequently may be the best approach to organizing an innovation team's work. More specifically, **establish guidance while keeping some lack of structure** in the organization; kind of an organized chaos, if you like. This can be challenging.

Think about a start-up: You start, and you have two people working hard night and day, chatting all the time and solving issues as they come. You grow, and you start adding employees. You get financing, and you start adding governance. Then you grow fast and unexpectedly, and you think that what you need to do is add processes and policies. And before you know it, the organization has become this heavy machine where processes, policies, and layers of management are killing innovation and simple sensible workflows (sounds familiar?). And then you decide you need some training, so you travel the world to attend presentations and workshops and come across the latest trends in management. Or you bring in a consulting firm, which of course will try to sell something new, or at least something that appears to be new. And while this is happening, innovation is not happening.

According to our framework, the solution is not putting more processes in place or jumping on some new management bandwagon. Instead, you should set clear rules to start with – at times, very basic rules – and then let the system organize itself.

In our interview, **Victoria Vallström (Bastide)** shared her view on establishing processes to develop innovative ideas. According to her, unstructured work does not necessarily mean that there is no process involved. Instead, unstructured work can be done when you understand that when you're dealing with uncertainty, you cannot analyze and predict everything all the time. In this case, you have to probe and react, which is less structured than having the certainty of a step-by-step process to follow.

This sounds familiar. As part of this research, we interviewed **Stephen Simpson,** who established the Charles Perkins Centre (CPC) at the University of Sydney. The CPC has more than 1,500 researchers, educators, and practitioners from a diverse range of fields, including science, philosophy, and engineering. CPC was created to address the burden of chronic disease. It has been designed as a complex adaptive system, not as a bureaucratic machine (note, the center is also sheltered from the rest of the University in terms of operations as well as physical location).

In an article, Simpson explained in detail his thinking behind the design of the CPC:[11]

> Complex adaptive systems have been the greatest solvers of **hyper-complex problems** in the history of the known universe. Evolution by natural selection has given rise to the **wonders and diversity** of life-forms that populate our planet; **modifiable interactions** between nerve cells give **rise to the complex computing powers of brains** and to the emergence of consciousness, and interactions between genes, signaling molecules and cells in the embryo ultimately give rise to the fully formed organism through the processes of development. How better, then, to tackle the complex issues of chronic disease than by **building a complex adaptive research and education ecosystem?**

If you want this richness in collaboration and innovation, one way is to imitate natural systems. By following natural systems, Simpson emphasizes the importance of avoiding set processes and instead allowing evolution to guide the course of your path. Simpson explains:

It is the same set of principles that empowers individual nerve cells in a brain to ultimately have conscious thoughts without any nerve cell knowing anything about anything else, or cells within a developing embryo giving rise to a newborn child that works perfectly without any cell knowing anything beyond its local environment necessarily ... You cannot have a blueprint for this.

Often events in the world occur without a plan or guided process, and it is important to take advantage of these "natural" moments to successfully develop an innovative idea. To achieve this goal, the CPC has been designed according to 12 principles, boundary conditions, and a framework. Explore the 12 principles and see how they can be applied to your own organization. Here we want to focus on the framework, which comprises the CPC strategy organized around four domains and six themes. Instead of organizing CPC around diseases, as is usual for such a research center, Simpson has organized it around four domains that define disciplinary areas: population health, biology of disease processes, society and environments, and a domain called "solutions," which provides the translational flow of the center. "Solutions" connects the other three domains.

In addition, there are six cross-cutting themes that intersect the four domains: (a) nutrition, (b) physical activity, exercise, and energy expenditure, (c) sleep, (d) Aboriginal and Torres Strait Islander health, (e) policy, governance, and ethics, and (f) integrative systems and modeling. The framework is then populated by 67 project nodes.[12]

Another perspective on vagueness is shared by **Carlo Gasparini**, Design Manager at Alessi, the Italian company behind some of the world's most iconic housewares and kitchen items. He emphasizes the importance of the "borderline," a line of vagueness between ideas that are possible in the future and ideas that are impossible and may never be understood. According to him, by staying near this vague line, one can find inspiration to develop innovative ideas. Rather than following a process, Gasparini encourages innovators to remain close to the borderline. To complicate things, the borderline is not visible. You cannot define it by market research. You can only discover it by taking risks. By taking risks and being willing to fail and try again, individuals will have much more success in their innovation journey, even if it takes time. If, on the other hand, individuals choose to follow a strict process, they may reach a dead end by restricting themselves. In return, they may never make it to the "borderline" where innovative ideas are most likely to be found.

The **second principle** within the "Promote Guided Vagueness" block calls on you to **help people collaborate prolifically**. The team needs to be exposed to boundless ideas. Note that this does not mean that the team innovates. Often the "Aha!" moment is very often still an individual one, but it happens only once individuals have exposure to ideas they can play with. Collaboration here is about creating the knowledge that then can be used to create insights.

In our interview with **Christine Ng**, Principal Engineer at General Mills, who leads the technology development in food ingredient and process systems to deliver innovative food product experiences to consumers, we discussed how to instil a collaborative environment within a company. According to her, many people tend to work in their own self-interest unless they are given a reason not to. Incentives to reach a certain outcome can be very powerful in convincing individuals to share their ideas with others in ways that benefit the team rather than competing against one another.

Incentives overall are a very tricky subject. In the book entitled *One Small Step Can Change Your Life: The Kaizen Way*, Robert Maurer, Director of Behavioral Sciences for the Family Practice Residency Program at Santa Monica UCLA Medical Center and a faculty member with the UCLA School of Medicine, talks about the *Kaizen* approach. Originally a Japanese word, kaizen is both about using small steps to improve a habit, process, or a product and about using very small moments to inspire creation of new products and inventions. The interesting point here is the importance of small prizes rather than big ones in order to provide motivation. Big cash rewards in the corporate world become a goal in itself and kill employees' natural desire to find stimulation and creativity in the world. But also, after these large prizes are introduced, they soon lose their novelty, and the desired behavioral change disappears. This is particularly evident when we compare what has happened in the US and Japan. In the US, large cash prizes are offered to employees who suggest ideas that will save the company money. In Japan, very small prizes are offered and, in companies such as Toyota, the person with the best idea over the course of a year will receive a Presidential Award in a formal ceremony and a fountain pen. Toyota receives 1.5 million suggestions a year and 95% are put into practice.[13] Recognition rather than material gains is what matters.

When it comes to collaboration, **Céline Le Cotonnec**, Chief Data Officer at AXA Singapore, emphasizes the importance of external sources to gain inspiration. Her company has recognized the benefits of receiving advice from outside sources in order to encourage innovative thinking and adaption, so they have continued to provide their employees with access to these sources. For example, they frequently organize inspirational talks by inviting an innovator from another company or another industry.

Paul Slezak also suggests that advice be taken from external individuals who are unfamiliar with the history of the (innovation) project. He suggests asking someone from outside, who has no knowledge of an innovation journey's history, what they would do. By introducing fresh eyes to a project, they may be able to develop new ideas that the internal team had not considered due to their fixation on their previous progress.

The **third principle** is to **focus firmly on objectives and avoid overly rigid KPIs**. Of course, innovators should be held accountable. But applying standard (corporate) practices is not appropriate for innovation. Pretty much across the board, our expert interviewees voiced concerns with companies putting too much emphasis on KPIs. According to **Stephen Simpson,** KPIs manage underperformance rather than celebrating innovation and success. Similarly, **Cindy Tripp**, design thinking expert and former key evangelist in starting Procter & Gamble's design thinking journey, stresses those responsible for innovation can't be expected to abide by the same measures of performance as others in the organization. If you have been given a cost budget to work to, do your best to stick to that. If you have been given a learning outcome to achieve (or a failure outcome for that matter), then focus on that. It's the focus on innovation – or lack thereof – that is making KPIs either encourage successful innovation journeys or stand in the way.

To these points, **André Teixeira**, entrepreneur and consultant and former Coca-Cola and other Fast Moving Consumer Goods companies veteran in various roles, including innovation, came up with a revolutionary idea to manage and evaluate innovation. He calls it the **Virtual Profit & Loss (P&L)**. Since most innovation fails, he suggests forgetting about measuring return on investment (ROI) or net present value (NPV). Measuring the impact of innovation is important, and asking whether the effort is worth it is valid. The critical distinction is when to bring these to the fore, because when you have not gone much further than ideation, measuring returns is, according to Teixeira, "an exercise in futility." Likewise, the underlying assumption of common return measurements is that a certain product is going to exist for several years (if not forever). However, this can hardly be said about most innovation, not least in this age of rapid changes, especially in the consumer goods industry – Teixeira's background – where product lifecycles can be short, sometimes not lasting more than a few months. He argues for the virtual P&L, which allows for failure in innovation as part of the process and accepts that, in innovation, success is the exception.

What does a virtual P&L look like? The virtual P&L is a company within a company, where the whole innovation team of the company is a shareholder. In fact, **André Teixeira** has first-hand experience with this concept. He has implemented the idea so that each time his team successfully launches an innovative product, they take a small royalty, which they use as revenue. He uses the revenue and costs in the virtual P&L to give his team bonuses.

Block 3: build momentum

- Principle 1: accept that innovation is cumulative and you might only recognize it ex post facto
- Principle 2: focus on learning through rapid validation
- Principle 3: proactively tap into experience from past failures

Why do we need to build innovation teams with the idea of momentum, with speed? In innovation, failure is pervasive – you can't innovate without taking risks. But to innovate, you need to do things differently, and these are often things done in ways that have not been proven yet. If you test quickly, you have the ability to test all assumptions and learn. It's about weeding out bad options, options that will clearly not work out upon implementation, rather than waiting for everyone to come on board on a visionary idea.

That is also why most successful innovators do not usually write long strategic plans. They don't research for half a year, and discuss for another. If they did, by the time they had the go-ahead to implement, ten competitive start-ups would have already entered the market. To engage in innovation, they adopt a piecemeal approach. Because they also understand that it is much harder to sell a complete idea than take people along to develop the idea together. In essence, "show and then tell" should be the mantra. But do it small to start with. Go for quick wins and then move on. Keep moving forward.

Consider Airbnb. Although it didn't start in a corporate setting, the principles apply just the same. Its first pitch deck is freely available online.[14] It is short and to the point, with each word very carefully selected to convey meaning. It focuses on the business model, and its go-to market plan is focused on actions and next steps rather than big visions. It also uses the 10/20/30 rule from Guy Kawasaki: 10 slides, 20 minutes, 30 point font.[15]

In a corporate setting this means that when you ask for money, don't write an essay for a million dollar pilot, write a one pager for a small test. If you have to spend time writing a full report on something that you don't even know works, or you need a consulting company to help, then the idea is not an innovative idea. Innovative ideas don't have support (see also the discussion on reliability versus validity by Cindy Tripp). Innovative ideas are fundamentally hypotheses, guesses of future value creation and capture. You don't need more than a page to put them into words, nor more than a few thousand dollars to truly test them.

Being brief has the added advantage of making you think about the concept harder, choose the words carefully, and use as much and no more than what you really need to say to convince people to help you test your hypothesis.

This is very much in line with the idea of the learning curve. The sooner you start, the sooner you will have the opportunity to learn, fail, improve, and do things better – particularly with respect to the competition. If you wait for the big pilot plant, you won't improve fast enough. Someone else with a nimble organization, whether start-up or larger corporate, will come around and beat you.[16]

So with respect to building momentum, the **first principle** underscores that you need to **accept that innovation is cumulative,** and you might only recognize it ex post facto.[17] **Victoria Vallström (Bastide)** from Lifesum argues that innovative ideas do not come from a genius who comes up with a grand idea. Instead they are cumulative and therefore only recognized as innovative in hindsight. You do not know you have created something groundbreaking until you go out and test it. In **Paul Slezak**'s experience, sometimes it's the very small ideas that have had a big impact on the business. Hence, he calls on innovators not to discount things a priori (i.e., without empirical evidence) because they seem small or because they are coming from out of left field. It's by testing an idea that you might end up realizing the impact on the bottom line.

It is one thing to acknowledge the (sometimes harsh) reality of innovation in theoretical terms. But when you engage in it yourself, it can become a whole different challenge. Knowing that innovation comes at the price of frequent setbacks, we may be biased toward saying yes to a lot of things in order to increase our odds. However, in many large organizations, there are plenty of people who will say no or put obstacles in the way of getting things done. How do we deal with that?

This is where the **second principle** comes into play: the **focus on learning through rapid validation**, not success or perfection.[18] According to most of the innovators in this book, it is important to be open about this from the outset. **Cindy Tripp** encourages potential innovators to seek feedback quickly. She believes that it is necessary to discuss one's idea with others before continuing to move forward. Bouncing ideas off other people really works. Individuals from the outside of the original plan development may provide a set of fresh eyes and helpful insights that create a better product.[19]

Trying things out with customers, whether it's a prototype[20] or a real product, is key to gaining momentum and a characteristic of many successful companies. Consider Amazon, for example, the behemoth in e-commerce. It is well known as a leader in innovation.[21] Why? Because of experimentation. Jeff Bezos is personally involved in selecting the projects that might bubble up from anywhere in the company. Experiments may start small and then grow over time. In the end, they will save a great deal of time and money. Other companies focus on trying things out internally, as Alessi does, to test new products with their people. In their case, a key element is a very well-developed matrix for evaluating products at a deep level (getting to the meanings of the product, rather than purely function).

In addition to learning by validating assumptions sooner rather than later, you can benefit greatly from looking backward. In other words, if applicable, do not discard but **proactively tap into experience from past failures**; this is the **third principle** within the "Build Momentum" block. Here, we specifically refer to acquiring insights from past efforts *within* your organization or even your team. You don't always have to start from scratch. Your organization may already have learnings that can fast-track your own innovation journey.

For example, **Christine Ng** always tries to seek out expert knowledge within General Mills early. She values the input of subject matter experts who know the history of a product or idea. They can share their experiences, such as problems encountered in the past or questions that have previously been asked and answered. She talks about the dangers of "reinventing the wheel," which sometimes you actually have to do, as the world has changed and it might now be ready to accept ideas that in the past were rejected. The more you are familiar with past efforts, the better equipped you are to sell the story in a more effective way.

Obviously, not all organizations are as large and equipped with experts as General Mills. But regardless, in-house expertise should be considered, if possible. This is particularly so during the ideation phase, where such anecdotal insights and lessons learned in the past can be of tremendous value. This may even add towards building consensus over time.

Notes

1 This is important. When we say "taste," we really mean two things. First, everyone in your organization should be familiar with who the customer is, what she or he wants from your products, and how your own products work. The reality is that your company might have amazing finance and accounting people who have been hired because of their amazing background, but they have never ever used your products or become familiar with them. So how can these people really understand the value of innovation and support it? How can they understand things from the customer perspective? Second, everyone should have an experimental mindset. We will discuss this further when we talk about the need to be built for speed.

2 See Rogers, E. M. (2010). *Diffusion of Innovations*: Simon & Schuster.

3 Baghai, M., Coley, S., & White, D. (2000). *The Alchemy of Growth*. Reading, MA: Basic Books. This is very much related to the idea of ambidexterity and the fact that executives need to take care of both execution (for short term profitability) and exploration of new opportunities (for long-term survival). For an introduction, see Harreld, J. B., O'Reilly III, C. A., & Tushman, M. L. (2007). Dynamic capabilities at IBM: Driving strategy into action. *California Management Review, 49*(4), 21–43.

4 For an in-depth discussion on archetypes of companies' engagement with start-ups, see Weiblen, T., & Chesbrough, H. W. (2015). Engaging with start-ups to enhance corporate innovation. *California Management Review, 57*(2), 66–90.

5 There is growing scepticism about some headline approaches. The Silicon Valley entrepreneur, Steve Blanks, author of four well-known books and the mind behind the Customer Development Methodology, writes in his blog: "most corporate/agency innovation processes funnel 'innovations' into 'demo days' or 'shark tanks' where they face an approval/funding committee that decides which innovation ideas are worth pursuing. However, without any measurable milestones to show evidence of the evolution of what the team has learned about the validity of the problem, customer needs, pivots, etc., the best presenter and flashiest demo usually win." See https://bit.ly/2SIu9nn.

6 See the podcast from Sydney Business Insight here: http://sbi.sydney.edu.au/innovation-centres-undermine-innovative-thinking/ and the original article in https://www.afr.com/brand/boss/do-innovation-centres-kill-innovation-20170714-gxbd3d. Ella Hafermalz, The performative office: A multi-case problematization of remote working, PhD Thesis, The University of Sydney Business School. Available here: https://ses.library.usyd.edu.au/handle/2123/15565.

7 See http://sbi.sydney.edu.au/innovation-centres-undermine-innovative-thinking/ and the original article in https://www.afr.com/brand/boss/do-innovation-centres-kill-innovation-20170714-gxbd3d.

8 See http://sbi.sydney.edu.au/innovation-centres-undermine-innovative-thinking/.

9 Great starting point for examples is Weiblen and Chesbrough, ibid.

10 Going even further, consider team diversity. We often hear about the need for diverse teams – from educational background to gender and country of origin – and more recently research is starting to acknowledge that diversity is also about chronotype diversity: some people have peak performance in the morning and some others later in the day. See https://www.businessinsider.com.au/design-your-work-schedule-sleep-chronotypes-2018-12.

11 See Simpson, S. J. (2017). A systems approach to public health. *Journal and Proceedings of the Royal Society of New South Wales, 150*(463/464), 61–67.

12 The structure of CPC is also discussed here: https://sydney.edu.au/charles-perkins-centre/our-research/research-strategy.html.

13 See Maurer, R. (2014). *One Small Step Can Change Your Life: The Kaizen Way*: Workman Publishing.

14 https://www.businessinsider.com.au/airbnb-a-13-billion-dollar-start-ups-first-ever-pitch-deck-2011-9.

15 See Kawasaki, G. (2015). *The Art of the Start 2.0*. Portfolio.
16 Learning from disruptive innovation theory remains relevant. Disruptive innovation theory, cursed but also blessed, makes you realize that things presented to you today might be inferior but might improve rapidly over time if the team behind them has an experimental mindset. The key questions to ask yourself are "Does it have the potential to catch up?" and "What is the team doing that makes them learn faster than competitors?"
17 This view of innovation as cumulative reminds us of another view on innovation. Kaizen and innovation have been discussed as two major strategies people use to create change. In his popular book, Robert Maurer says that innovation demands shocking and radical reforms, whereas Kaizen asks for small, comfortable steps towards improvements. In the end, both approaches lead to changes, but they play with the mind in a very different way. Sometimes thinking about innovation is daunting, as a large goal may create fear for some people; the brain's response is to shut down creativity. Kaizen, using small steps to improve a product, process, or habit, or using very small moments to inspire new products and inventions, will help the human mind to overcome the fear that blocks success and creativity. See Maurer, R. (2014). *One Small Step Can Change Your Life: The Kaizen Way*. New York, NY: Workman Publishing.
18 Should companies have a Chief Experiments Officer? http://www.theinnovations-cout.com/c-e-o-the-new-chief-experiments-officer-leads-innovation/.
19 We could expand on this at length, but essentially it means **applying the scientific method** constantly. That will make you focus on what should be done in order to have speed.

1. **Observe** what's going on around you and absorb what's coming out of the sensing mechanisms that have been established within the company as well as the user research.
2. **Create hypotheses –** really guesses – about why things are happening in a certain way or where new value creation opportunities are.
3. **Experiment** to test your hypotheses. Use the least amount of resources possible. The key is learning, not perfection.
4. **Measure** the results to evaluate and decide whether you are right or not. If you are right, it's time to ask for more money and scale.

20 As in Design Sprints. See "Resources" in Part 3.
21 https://www.vox.com/new-money/2016/12/28/13889840/amazon-innovation-google-apple.

5

BUILDING BLOCKS FOR INNOVATION

The Frontier

By now you have completed the Core. You have a new organizational design that is geared towards innovation. You have established a guided vagueness approach so that the right people have the right incentives and goals while letting go of the idea that we must be able to predict everything. And finally, you have adopted a bias for action and are built for speed so new ideas can be tested quickly and inexpensively.

Now we move on to where the real work begins, where ideas really emerge. This is where we go from a great idea that has been tested with quick and inexpensive tests to developing it into an actual project. Here at the Frontier, we search for anomalies and surprising things that we transform into hypotheses about the future and test them. The building blocks of innovation in the Frontier will provide the conceptual foundation to put this into practice.

Block 4: sense the world

- Principle 1: create and explore intersections, because that's where innovation happens
- Principle 2: don't imitate your competitors unless you want to fall behind
- Principle 3: encourage co-creation to evolve ideas

Sometimes when we think about innovation we think about Steve Jobs or Jonathan Ive. We consider lonely geniuses who spent their time searching for inspiring experiences. We characterize them as fundamentally curious and intensely focused. These legendary innovators absorbed as much as they could from the external environment, not sheltering themselves from it. Once they have an inspiring idea, they are laser-focused in executing it.

How can we accommodate creative geniuses? What feeds them? Where do ideas come from?

Fundamentally, the key to transforming ideas to reality is good data points. You need to have made proper observations about the world around you, about technologies being developed in university laboratories, and about culture and society. You can't make a good decision unless you have the facts in front of you; similarly, you can't create an amazing new product, service, or business model unless you have "sensed" the world around you.

And that's where processes and procedures are invaluable to creating the new. You need good data. The "Aha!" moment[1] most often happens when you least expect it, when you're taking a shower or walking in the park. But that genius moment happens after you have filled up your brain with good stuff.[2] To do that, you need to have a process and systems in place so that the good stuff is sensed and then placed where you need it.[3]

Before we proceed with the principles, we need to make one point very clear. It is impossible to be an innovator, a front runner, if you only spend time with people similar to you, whether that is in gender, age, function, or industry. Sociologists call this homophily, and it has deep implications for innovators because it limits the information people receive, the attitudes they form, and the interactions they experience over their life.[4] So, for example, you think spending time with start-ups will benefit your innovation journey. But what will you gain from this? You will only learn about that start-up. You have denied yourself the opportunity to sense what's going on in the broader context. Understanding the future of any industry is based on first sensing and then making use of available data. In this way, you will be engaging early, ahead of the game, and gain competitive advantage.

But early engagement isn't enough – if it was, all those large companies that set up incubators or accelerators would have become top innovators. Too often, these end up as purely marketing activities. You need to think differently from the rest in order to be novel, new, and innovative. You need to follow other kinds of stuff, to seek out other kinds of inputs and inspirations. And you need to be part of the conversation at the very beginning in order to slowly, over time, absorb the cues that are presented to you, make sense, recognize and form patterns, and come up with your hypotheses about the world. Research on opportunity generation looks at the importance of being part of the conversation and the ecosystem in order to be innovative; it's also a theme that recurs in our interviews.[5]

The **first principle** calls on aspiring innovators to **create and explore intersections of existing ideas, because that's where innovation happens**. A consistent theme across our interviews is that innovation is often putting together things from different parts of life. The creation of something new is often purely the result of combining two things that already exist but in different contexts. When we say "life" or "context" we mean these in the broadest sense. They are not necessarily related to work. Often, it's when you are travelling or attending an exhibition or playing a sport that you realize that a similar problem has been solved in a way that differs from the approach you would have undertaken in your day job. You start thinking: what if we use the same principle to solve a problem at work?

In other words, an innovative idea does not just happen in a vacuum. Fundamentally, innovation is about novel ideas, not necessarily big ideas. Novel ideas are usually a recombination of things, hence the intersection. Elon Musk observed that many fresh solutions are the results of cross-fertilization of ideas from different domains. He said: "A lot of people who spend a long time trying to figure out how to solve tough problems in one industry don't ask, 'Well, is there some other way we could apply that solution to a different industry?'... And that can be really, really powerful."[6]

André Teixeira considers the intersection between different disciplines in order to gain inspiration. He tries to expose himself to concepts that are at the intersection of science and technology with cognitive, sensorial, psychological, and other aspects of the overall human experience. By considering multiple disciplines and their connections, the world can be conceived of and viewed in a new way. These connections can then be solidified through the development of a disruptive product or process. The idea of crossroads and connections between ideas from different industries is key also in the interviews with Céline Le Cotonnec, Peter Löfgren, Christine Ng, Tim Romero, and Carlo Gasparini.[7]

In particular, for **Carlo Gasparini** and the work at Alessi, the intersection happens at two levels: First, the design of objects that have a fundamental function (a juicer) is viewed in terms of art (hence, Alessi juicers can be found in museums around the world). The research behind the concepts is based on culture and trends rather than usability, unlike the approach of design thinking (e.g., remember the sweet spot of innovation for IDEO). Second, who designs the objects is key. It is not necessarily a designer; in fact, in several instances, architects are the designers. They bring a different scale to the problem at hand and, as such, a different type of creativity. Hence, the intersections can be created either by using individuals with very different backgrounds,[8] at least in the research phase, or by the same individuals with very diverging interests, as in the case of André Teixeira and his deep knowledge of innovation, philosophy, and the chemistry of food, and Stefan Vlachos and his disparate interests.

Combining concepts from different realms is one thing. But will it make a difference if it is perfectly in line with your industry peers? Most probably not. This leads us to the **second principle:** if you **follow your competitors, you will never be an innovator**. You can make improvements, but that's not really being innovative. Instead, by setting up so-called sensing mechanisms, you can monitor and feed back insights to your organization.

How do you do that? First, you have to identify what to sense. Previous work by one of the authors[9] has synthesized academic work with the views of executives on how they sense the environment. Some of the recurring themes they identified are as follows:

1. Internal R&D labs
2. Processes to identify target market needs
3. Processes to identify science and technology development
4. Processes to tap suppliers and complementors' innovation

There are two things to note. The first is that in (2) we talk especially about culture and the influence of culture on consumer needs and tastes. Here we are not talking about large-sample, marketing studies of consumer behavior. By the time that consumers are able to express their needs and likes, it's usually too late for innovators. As in the case of Alessi, **Carlo Gasparini** shows how the starting point of their process is inspiration from culture, not from market research. Only once they have identified a "dream to focus on," do they come down from the clouds and define the product that can satisfy such a dream. The second is that of the four themes, none addresses competitors. Again, this is because by the time you observe competitors' behaviors, you've missed the boat on innovation.[10]

The **third principle** is about encouraging some sort of, sometimes loose, **co-creation to evolve ideas,** whether it is at the workshop level or by participating in conversations that take place outside your organization. Several innovators spoke to us about the importance of talking with various stakeholders to understand problems that are perhaps latent, or to generate solutions that rely on the expertise of the stakeholder.

How do you do it? Here are some ideas.

Mark Nierwetberg talks about **co-creation with stakeholders** via workshops that are loosely structured to present some technology to the potential client but in reality creating an outlet for the potential client to develop awareness of some of his or her challenges. Don't assume that you know the problem – because you don't – or at least you don't know it from the perspective of the "problem owner." You might know the technology, because you own it, but the urgent problem to solve is ultimately revealed in the conversation.

An example of this is shared by **Peter Löfgren** of ABB's innovation hub SynerLeap. ABB is a leading technology company in the fields of power grids, automation, and robotics. The latter has been of particular benefit to a start-up, the "problem owner," that is trying to change the way professional runners train. The start-up could have worked alone and eventually figured things out. Most likely, this would have taken a long time, and competitors might have been quicker to market. However, ABB with its deep expertise in motor technology and robotics was able to offer a solution, because it works with both motors and robots – the very solution needed by the problem owner. In doing so it was able to accelerate innovation, in a way that was both new and exciting, and completely disruptive. According to Löfgren, it is a prime example of the value generated within the ecosystem.

André Teixeira offers another example. He points out that consumers only know what they want now, so their opinions, or those of other collaborations, may only be the starting point of the innovation – they can't offer a solution or sometimes even identify the benefit of the solution you offer them.[11] One way to overcome this is to have "informants" around the major trend-setting capitals of the world to feed you with insights. These four capitals could be Tokyo, Paris, London, and New York.[12] From fashion trends to mobile app adoption, these are places where things happen before other places. If you have access to this information before competitors, then you have the chance to develop insights for value creation. We know of other companies that have similar approaches – for instance, **Céline Le Cotonnec's** example of her dedicated foresight team. Similarly, there are service providers, such as Berlin-based HYPERMORGEN, who are ready to fill that gap and help (mostly) corporates get a better understanding about the future by leveraging their close ties to R&D and start-up ecosystems, and because they are continuously scanning the environment for the next innovative frontier (and beyond).

Something everyone should borrow from the *Power of Pull*[13] is to send your people out to sense the environment at what they call the Edge. A common approach is for a company to send a high-performing engineer to an engineering conference where he or she meets like-minded people and perhaps presents the latest stuff from your own business. But what does your engineer learn there? What can he or she bring back? Some insights about what your competitors are doing right now. Nothing that will help you stay ahead of the innovation curve. You need to send them to some conferences where they will understand a fair bit of what is going on, but it's not necessarily their domain. In this way, they will gain insights into something new and hopefully have the opportunity to translate them in their daily jobs.

But let's also consider **Alessi** once again. They have a very special approach that relies on the sense-making ability of the designers they engage with rather than the customers. In innovation, Alessi's view is that the first important step is to succeed in "interpreting" innovative ideas.

A caveat: We argue that when you follow competitors, it does not necessarily make you an innovator. We stand by that. In reality, though, analogical reasoning can become a very powerful assistant when you follow companies that are trying to solve the same customer problem that you are trying to solve. A powerful example is that of Apple's iTunes/iPod as a combination of Walkman and Napster. This is a story from one of our favorite books by John Mullins and Randy Komisar.[14] Entrepreneurs can develop new business ideas by looking at success stories from other companies or industries, that is, what has worked for others in the past. On the other hand, even so-called failures can be turned into useful insights. If you study why something or someone did not succeed, you are already one step ahead of making the same mistakes. (Recall principle 3, "Proactively tap into experience from past failures," of the "Build Momentum" block.)

For instance, consider the iPod. In retrospect, one could argue that there had been a very iconic success story already: Sony's Walkman. It was easy for Apple to see that people were willing to pay for a device that allows them to listen to music on the go because it had been proven already by the Sony Walkman. The validation had already been done. But they also had a failure to follow: Napster. Founded in 1999, Napster quickly grew into one of the most popular peer-to-peer music-sharing sites. The problem was that most of the content was copyrighted and hence sharing was illegal. The creation of a legitimate alternative was obvious, at least in hindsight. And that is precisely what Apple set out to do with the launch of the iTunes store after Napster ran into trouble. Apple created an online store where people could download and save music after paying a small fee to avoid legal issues.

So when you are sensing for ideas, consider reframing the competitor analysis and instead call it a systematic process of reviewing successes and failures in innovation.

Block 5: extract meanings

- Principle 1: stay close to your customers, but not too close
- Principle 2: create new meanings for your customers, not just new value
- Principle 3: hire for passion, not just skills or knowledge

Customers are kings and queens. Gone are the days in which a company sells an updated version of a package while the product is the same. Nowadays customers know the difference between an innovative phone, and a slightly tweaked version of the same phone. Managers and entrepreneurs alike talk about human-centered design and the need to focus on customers' wants and needs. First and foremost, you need to solve a customer pain point. To do so, you can draw from a methodological repository that is rich and plentiful – from design thinking to ethnography to prototyping to all of the above.

But true success lies not just in solving a customer problem. Innovation is not about blindly applying a step-by-step process to understand a specific customer need in a specific context, a journey that goes from A to B. It's much, much more. The following three principles derived from our interviewees' personal experience illustrate this.

First, we encourage you to **use aspects of design thinking or even lean methods but go beyond that**, the first principle within the "Extract Meanings" block. In essence, true innovators go beyond the key tools of design thinking, such as user experience, user centricity, human-centered design, and journey mapping. They reflect more deeply on how to delight the customer. While these design thinking tools allow you to participate in the game of innovating, they are not enough to win anymore, because in times of constant change, your customers today are not necessarily the same customers tomorrow.

Think of Henry Ford's famous quote in which he says, if you ask your customers what they want, they simply tell you "a faster horse." Likewise, Steve Jobs insisted that Apple products not be developed using focus groups. Why? Because customers don't know what they want.

Indeed, focus groups can be dangerous. First of all, they are prone to suffer from groupthink and confirmation bias: you just say whatever everyone else is saying and whatever it takes to please the researchers, so you get your money and go home. A strategic designer with whom we have worked, Angela Mayer, explains the value or lack thereof of focus groups to identify user needs and wants:

Focus groups versus design research approaches are akin to the difference between a visit to the zoo and going on safari. You might go to the zoo and see the elephants there, and you would get a sense of what elephants are like. There might be a group of them in the enclosure, and you can watch them eat and drink a bit, but they'll generally just be standing around, not really doing anything. In fact, one behavior you might observe is seeing them swaying back and forth. Your big takeaway might be that swaying back and forth is an essential elephant behavior.

But contrast that experience to viewing elephants on safari (the analog to doing ethnographic research) and you'll see a much broader array of elephant behaviors, across a range of habitats. You'll come away with a much richer sense of elephant behavior and probably learn a lot about a whole range of their habits. But one insight you won't come away with is the insight about elephants swaying while they stand in place, because it turns out, that's something elephants only do in captivity. So with the zoo (focus group) there's a big risk of drawing the wrong conclusions, based on the artificiality of that situation, and the fact that a focus group is a forced conversation and not a real-life observation.

But what should you do instead? Design thinking and user-centered design have created a massive shift in the way that companies think about their work, offering a shift away from technology-driven products and an obsession with quality and replicability (see **Cindy Tripp's** interview).[15] Instead, talking about users and needs through observations and interviews has become common.

Jeanne Marell, the Head of User Research at Coloplast, who took a similar stance on using consumers' opinions for innovation development, warns that consumers give feedback based on how they are here and now; in other words, they can't project into the future, nor can they predict the possibilities that may come from innovation. Thus, understanding your customers' wants and needs is great, but not enough. This is particularly the case in industries where product development can take significant time because if there is a considerable lag between your talking to customers and deriving insights, the world may have moved on. According to Marell, a better approach is to focus on users of *adjoining* products to understand trends. How are they behaving? What do they seek in a product? Where can you spot changes in attitude? This once again illustrates the importance of establishing sensing mechanisms that go beyond your immediate competitive environment and instead engage with the edge.

You should also go the extra mile when articulating the quintessential impact of a proposed innovation. In other words, seek to **create new, current, and forward-looking meaning for customers, not only value**, the second principle within the "Extract Meanings" block. Meaning goes beyond value. Innovation is meaning. If you create meaning, you have products that have long lives. Technology is sexy. Adding a new feature, for example, a faster processor, is good, but that doesn't create true, forward-looking meaning.

The drawback of a simple journey-mapping approach is this: identifying your customers' pain points and providing an improved service will help you foster incremental innovation but not innovation that really changes the way customers get their jobs done.

Roberto Verganti, the scholar behind the idea of Design Driven Innovation, spent a large part of his life studying the so-called Italian Design Factories such as Alessi (see the interview with **Carlo Gasparini**), B&B, and Oluce. He then spent another part of his life working in Scandinavia, another area very well known for design. In the Italian factories of design, new products and services do not come out of studying customers and how they use stuff, but from long-term studies on product meanings. In Scandinavia, a design orientation is part of the culture, the way everyone is brought up from a very early age. Homes are often preferred to bars and other public places for socializing, and much effort and money is put into *hygge*.[16] Together with Don Norman, one of the greatest design minds of our century,[17] Verganti suggests that when you give someone something and you study what they do with it and ways to improve it, you climb a hill of incremental innovation. You can give them faster or more user-friendly tools, but in the end you are still on the same hill. If you want to jump on another hill, then you need either some new technological advances and/or a new meaning that you are creating for the customer. In both instances, at the beginning, the performance of the new product might not be as good as the old one, but over time that performance will improve by studying the customers and how to make the product better. Think about the Nintendo Wii. When it came out, it included some technological innovation (the MEMS accelerometer), but its great innovation was making gaming social, even for people who previously didn't play games. It involved the entire body and everyone could play, even your grandmother. That's when Nintendo took gaming from one hill to another.[18]

This aligns with what **Cindy Tripp** told us. Innovation is meaningful and useful. Too often we forget about the meaningful and focus on the useful, yet it is the meaningful that can make the difference between a product that sells for one year and a product that becomes an icon. Finding meaning is hard – it won't come out of a two-hour brainstorming session. It comes from deep investigations into cultures and trends. Hence, you may need to engage with ethnographers and interpreters of the world such as artists, filmmakers, and other creative people.

The third principle within the "Extract Meanings" block is that you should **hire people who are passionate and knowledgeable** when you set out to build an innovative organization. Hire people who embrace change and know how to make change. Underlying this, they need to be able to perform a function but to also understand your products. If they haven't played with your products in the first place, they won't know how to improve them. For example, in the past, when a company hired a CFO, the hiring team or board was looking for someone who knows finance and regulations inside out. Thus, the ideal candidate had to excel in that function. But nowadays, if you don't know your products and your customers, you can't make decisions that are meaningful in satisfying customers' needs and wants. Your view of the world is clouded by your background, such as finance, rather than understanding more broadly the mission of your company. The interview with **Mark Nierwetberg** was telling in this respect. He talked about openness in leadership development and recruiting in the telco industry – a CFO does not necessarily watch pay-per-view TV, yet knowing what is it and how it works should be key to the role.

Block 6: generate consensus

- Principle 1: accept the limits of ingrained practices such as brainstorming
- Principle 2: cultivate serendipity
- Principle 3: make selling an idea a critical part of the task, not an afterthought

Collaboration is key. True. We stressed this already in Part 1 but we can't stress it enough. By discussing "stuff" with people from different parts of the world, industries, experiences, and so on, you enrich your knowledge, see other points of view, and ultimately open yourself to inspiration. Different combinations of peoples and contexts generate different ideas. But which people and which contexts? Who decides which people are chosen? What makes the group more innovative than the individual? And in your company does "collaboration" just mean "workshops" and "brainstorming"? After all, some of the most innovative companies we have today were sparked by an idea from an individual person, such as Nike founder Phil Knight. Knight was in his mid-twenties when he started selling shoes out of his car at track meets. He had minimal resources to work with, but his initial idea grew into the multibillion-dollar shoe empire that we all know. Even in academic research, we still don't have a clear answer to the question about when a group is better than an individual in generating innovative ideas.

The **first principle** of "Generate consensus" is to **accept the limits of ingrained practices such as brainstorming.** Instead of fostering innovation, brainstorming sessions create an artificial environment that may block the formation of really innovative ideas (remember, innovative ideas are often hard to sell). As we said previously, many ideas come when we are doing something else, like showering or walking in the park. Making idea a creation a "job" that takes place in a "meeting" is not likely to lead to true innovation. Innovation comes from individual experience, struggle, and even failure. Thomas Edison is widely renowned as a pioneer of innovation, as he essentially designed a process for successfully moving ideas into commercialization. He used profits from his initial innovations to fund his own "hothouse for innovation," which is essentially the same concept as "incubation chambers" used by a number of organizations today. Edison did not come up with his brilliant inventions by having collaborative brainstorming sessions; instead, it was his individual experiences and failures that inspired his innovative ideas. Academic studies comparing the outcome of individuals working independently on a problem with that of the of teams working on the same problem using brainstorming techniques found that teams produce fewer and less diverse ideas than individuals. This may be because when people work together in the same room, they focus on a smaller number of concepts, and a few people may dominate, often by taking a negative stance toward new ideas.[19]

People working alone may be more likely to succeed in innovation – for example, Steve Jobs did not run brainstorming sessions.[20] In most cases, innovations begin in the mind of single individuals, but in order for these ideas to be realized they need to be developed by a collaboration of thinkers. In our interview, RecruitLoop CEO **Paul Slezak** stressed how any single individual within his company can (and has) come up with innovative and game-changing ideas once given the opportunity to speak up and share their own insights.

Brainstorming is a key practice within successful organizations, and it's easy to fall into habitual patterns of thinking even as we seek to generate new ideas. To help us better understand how the mind and body work together to keep ideas flowing, we spoke with Marco Beghin, an expert in the Alexander Technique, which is an educational process that teaches people to become aware of and change unhelpful habits of posture, breathing, and movement. Marco Beghin is the founder of Body Economics in Los Angeles, and spent several years as a marketing and product development executive at DēLonghi and was later President of Moleskine America.[21] We asked Marco whether in his experience he found a relationship between a tension-free body and creative thinking. We were interested in understanding whether slowing down could help us access our best ideas. He explained to us his observations in working with a variety of clients, from artists to corporate executives:

> In observations with my clients practicing the Alexander Technique, I have noticed a clear relationship between creative thinking and well-being. By slowing down the body, a new level of awareness can be explored in relation to our environment, the people we interact with, and our goals. Starting with quiet experiences – and pausing to notice – the senses become fully available, and we are allowed to feel whole, supported, coordinated, and curious to think and move in unfamiliar ways. New patterns of thinking can arise – the result of an integrated psychological/physical/emotional being in the process of creation – all through a process of embodied cognitive action.
>
> Before your next brainstorming session, try lying down for 5–10 minutes. Allow yourself to feel supported by the ground and give your weight to the floor. Stay open with your senses – eyes, ears, taste, smell, and touch. Observe the movement happening inside and around you. Don't interfere. Try speaking out loud whatever comes to mind from your body sensations. It might just be your best idea.

This takes us to the **second principle, cultivating serendipity**. Serendipity needs to be given space.[22] **Stephen Simpson**, the Director of the Charles

Perkins Centre, emphasizes the importance of serendipity and open-mindedness when trying to reach the "Aha!" moment, because ideas may come to you without searching. This view is shared by **Mark Nierwetberg** when he talks about open spaces and playfulness. By fixating on a specific area or process, innovators may have a difficult time remaining open to serendipity. Working in an area where you have little experience can lead to more open-mindedness, because too much expertise can lead to process fixation. **Stefan Vlachos** believes that being a beginner stimulates creativity because you are at the bottom of a steep learning curve.

Finally, the **third principle** calls on innovators to **make selling an idea to the relevant stakeholders a critical part of the task, not an afterthought**. A grand vision is simply not enough. It's not just about imagining a better future, improved products, or services. By definition, novel ideas embody something new, possibly something unthinkable and unheard of, and are therefore hard to sell.

The difficulty in selling innovative ideas is based on the difference between validity and reliability, which has been extensively explored by Roger Martin.[23] Reliability seeks to produce consistent, predictable outcomes by utilizing a system that is restricted to the use of objective data – for instance, predicting a customer's future purchases by using an extensive amount of data collected in your company's customer relations management software. Validity, on the other hand, seeks to produce outcomes that meet the desired objective, even if the system can't produce a consistent, predictable outcome. Both are in constant competition. You can increase reliability, but validity suffers. And vice versa.

Innovation lives in the world of validity, not reliability. For aspiring innovators, this means you cannot rely much on what you know today about your customers, market size, and so on to make hypotheses about what they will want in the future. Alessi, for instance, goes even further. They start from dreams and then decide upon the functionality of the product. And again, as discussed by **Carlo Gasparini**, the MAYA Principle really tells you to go step by step – don't sell the vision at the start but get people to accept the straightforward parts first, the parts that are closer to what they know at that point in time.

Stefan Vlachos talks about entertaining your audience by telling a journey story when pitching an innovative idea. He says that stories should include the different paths taken and the people met along the way. By allowing the audience to follow innovators on their journey and to relate to the individuals involved, they are more likely to become invested in the process and the product. Put simply, the audience establishes an emotional connection through the richness of the story. Interestingly, Stefan argues that the person who has crafted the story or even managed the innovation team does not necessarily have to be the one telling the story. In the hospital environment, for example, innovation should be pitched by a doctor, a nurse, or a physiotherapist because then it's much more credible.

Melissa Widner agrees that stories need to be told to get investors on board. She talks about passion and getting the audience to share the passion through powerful narratives. This is especially important if you are trying to get your idea to stand out in a sea of competing ideas and initiatives.

Keep in mind, however, that a one-size-fits-all approach won't work. You may need to tailor your story for different groups of people. **André Teixeira** talks about "pre-pitching," talking to the marketing team and the engineers and subtly massaging the story each time to bring out the nuances that are relevant to each audience. In this way, when you talk to the broader organization you can avoid the "yes-butters, those people that say, 'Yes, but you cannot do this'" because you've already got the specific areas of the business on board.

Here, we also think of what **Christine Ng** shared about pitching in particular. According to her, pitching an idea is not a moment in time, and most certainly not a meeting. Pitching an idea is a process. This is particularly important in solving complex problems, which may take years to develop into a fruitful outcome. She points out that you must bring the stakeholders along with you right from the start. If they feel like they are part of the solution they will always support it. And while trying to win over different people to support your idea, you should always bear in mind that even the most straightforward, compelling, or even logical initiatives need a solid narrative to be sold. **André Teixeira** talks about capturing the audience's imagination – because ultimately their job is to make money for the company now, not think about how to do it in an unimaginable future.

Indeed, at times, the constraints of the day-to-day business need to be acknowledged, and you may even need to take your foot off the accelerator. **Céline Le Cotonnec** underscores the necessity of providing some tangible benefits to other departments in the here and now in order to garner support for future innovative initiatives. She describes this as a trade-off because often the business is overloaded with what they have to do today.

By now, you should have a valuable overview of the key principles of innovation based on our framework and its two core elements. In Part 2 of the book, you will hear firsthand about the innovation practices of people successful in their field. How do they approach constant change? What is their perspective on innovation? What are their lessons learned? Where have they seen others (or themselves) run into roadblocks? The interviews are rich in anecdotes as well as practical advice for the aspiring innovator – that is, for you.

The future that lies ahead is up to you. With the *6 Building Blocks for Innovation* at hand, you are well equipped to start your innovation journey, or reinvigorate an existing one. Pick the blocks that are most relevant for your circumstances, perhaps those that will likely work best with your company, with your people, with your culture – or simply those where you see the greatest need to act. Test them, see what works, see what does not work, and think about how you can change what you are doing. Ultimately, your own interpretation of innovation will be the one that matters, the one that will shape the future of your business.

Notes

1 See Berns, G. (2010). *Iconoclast: A Neuroscientist Reveals How to Think Differently*: Harvard Business Press.

2 This is perhaps one of the greatest books about the importance of absorbing a broad amount of information from disparate sources: Hagel III, J., Brown, J. S., & Davison, L. (2012). *The Power of Pull: How Small Moves, Smartly Made, Can Set Big Things in Motion*. Philadelphia, PA: Basic Books.

3 Companies need systems to absorb and process information (sensing capabilities), which is then transformed into innovative ideas by a selected few (seizing capabilities), usually people at the top with a broad range of experiences and knowledge. See Dong, A., Garbuio, M., & Lovallo, D. (2016). Generative sensing: A design perspective on the microfoundations of sensing capabilities. *California Management Review, 58*(4), 97–117.

4 McPherson, M., Smith-Lovin, L., & Cook, J. M. (2001). Birds of a feather: Homophily in social networks. *Annual Review of Sociology, 27*(1), 415–444.

5 We could provide you citations from scientific studies but, in the end, this is very well explained from a practical perspective by Roberto Verganti and his work on the innovation coming out of the Italian Factories of Design as well as the work on ecosystems by Mariana Mazzucato in relation to the importance of companies co-location. See Verganti, R. (2009). *Design Driven Innovation: Changing the Rules of Competition by Radically Innovating What Things Mean*. Boston, MA: Harvard Business Press; Mazzucato, M. (2013). *The Entrepreneurial State: Debunking the Public vs. Private Myth in Risk and Innovation*. London, UK: Anthem.

6 See Elon Musk's conversation with Hal Gregersen about the importance of looking into solutions in other industries, reported in Gregersen, H. (2018). *Questions Are the Answer. A Breakthrough Approach to Your Most Vexing Problems at Work and in Life*: Harper Business.

7 When talking about the intersection of different domains, explicitly using analogical reasoning can help you transfer the properties of one domain into another.

8 When putting together a team, whether it is in sports or in business, you don't want to rely too much on one star player. You want to include different personalities and backgrounds. The different expertise and points of view might create some conflict, but that is necessary in order to innovate.

9 Dong et al., ibid.

10 Dong et al., ibid.

11 If you enter a co-creation session to present your understanding of the customer's issues but also bring an open mind (you're not just there to push your views), then a co-creation session can become very powerful.

12 A well-known strategy framework talks about companies at the top of their game in dynamic industries having developed so called sensing capabilities. Sensing capabilities involve sensing the environments for trends, whether behavioral trends, technology trends, etc., and developing insights into where the world is heading. Importantly, whereas the capability to develop insights is fundamentally bestowed upon individuals, the sensing process can be systematized. See Teece, D. J. (2007). Explicating dynamic capabilities: the nature and microfoundations of (sustainable) enterprise performance. *Strategic Management Journal, 28*(13), 1319–1350. See also: Dong et al., ibid. See also, on the importance of sensing, Hagel III, J., Brown, J. S., & Davison, L. (2012). *The Power of Pull: How Small Moves, Smartly Made, Can Set Big Things in Motion*. Philadelphia, PA: Basic Books.

13 Hagel III et al., ibid.

14 Mullins, J., & Komisar, R. (2009). *Getting to Plan B*. Boston, MA: Harvard Business Press.

15 Also, the larger the company, the more it hires for function. They hire an exceptional finance person or an exceptional marketing person. Very likely, these people don't

use the product and don't understand the customer. The move to design thinking, user centricity, and human-centered design that has taken place over the last 15–20 years has not happened in some companies.

16 Two enjoyable and informative readings about the importance of design in Danish lives are: Kingsley, P. (2012). *How to be Danish: A Journey to the Cultural Heart of Denmark*. New York, NY: Mable Arch Press; Wiking, M. (2016). *The Little Book of Hygge: The Danish Way to Live Well*: Penguin UK.

17 See Norman, D. A., & Verganti, R. (2014). Incremental and radical innovation: Design research vs. technology and meaning change. *Design Issues, 30*(1), 78–96.

18 Note here the similarity with disruptive innovation. Disruptive innovation, as discussed in Christensen's work, tells the story of how new entrants have displaced large incumbents in markets. One of the key points of his framework is around the idea that large incumbents are trying to please existing customers, often large customers, by providing always better-performing products along some well-known metrics (e.g. faster processors). New entrants cannot attract the same customers and so offer a product that redefines the metrics of performance. See here for the latest account of Christensen's framework in Christensen, C. M., Raynor, M. E., & McDonald, R. (2015). What is disruptive innovation. *Harvard Business Review, 93*(12), 44–53.

19 Mullen, B., Johnson, C., & Salas, E. (1991). Productivity loss in brainstorming groups: A meta-analytic integration. *Basic and Applied Social Psychology, 12*(1), 3–23; Kohn, N. W., & Smith, S. M. (2011). Collaborative fixation: Effects of others' ideas on brainstorming. *Applied Cognitive Psychology, 25*(3), 359–371.

When you work in teams in the same room, if there is not a high level of trust and an understanding that everyone's ideas are welcome no matter how crazy or simple they are, some people will not voice their opinions because of fear of judgment or ridicule. See also https://www.linkedin.com/pulse/science-shows-brainstorms-dont-work-why-do-we-still-use-dave-birss/ and Birss, D. (2018). *How to Get to Great Ideas: A System for Smart, Extraordinary Thinking*. London, UK: Nicholas Brealey Publishing.

20 See Schilling, M. A. (2018). *Quirky: The Remarkable Story of the Traits, Foibles, and Genius of Breakthrough Innovators who Changed the World*: PublicAffairs.

21 See www.bodyeconomics.com.

22 See https://www.nytimes.com/2013/04/07/opinion/sunday/engineering-serendipity.html.

23 See Martin, R. (2009). *The Design of Business: Why Design Thinking Is the Next Competitive Advantage*. Boston, MA: Harvard Business School Press.

PART II
Innovation in action

6

CARLO GASPARINI

The key to a good result depends very much on the personal understanding created between the various actors sharing the challenge and on the mutual trust placed in the relationship between designer and company.

Carlo Gasparini was born in Milan in 1985. He studied architecture at the Politecnico di Milano where, after graduating, he worked as a teaching and research assistant in computational design and digital fabrication. Before starting his collaboration with Alessi, he worked as an architect and design consultant for the marble producers' area in Carrara (Tuscany). At Alessi, as Design Manager in the Marketing Department, he leads the product development process, working between designers and technicians from concept to industrialization. His role aims to combine and mediate the dreams of creativity on the one hand and the market's and production's constraints on the other. He is also responsible for the Alessi design innovation agenda, and managing research projects and workshops in collaboration with other companies and with universities.

What is innovation to you?

Alessi, as defined by Alberto Alessi himself, is a research laboratory in the field of applied arts – a company devoted to research and aesthetic experimentation in home product design. Being innovative, or at least trying to be innovative, is part of our nature and many innovative ideas have been developed at Alessi over the course of its almost 100 years. Our *raison d'etre* constantly brings us to the exploration of new territories connected to the evolution of the customs and habits of contemporary society, with the intent of giving shape and matter to our times.

One could go into the merits of many of Alessi's innovative projects/products, from Richard Sapper's melodic kettle, which took three years to develop in search of the perfect melody, to Philippe Starck's unpredictable citrus juicer, which challenges the relationship between form and function, becoming a provocative design icon. However, I think that here the most interesting thing is not trying to make a list of examples but rather to talk about the innovative idea that underlies everything, the idea that laid the foundations for industrial success, allowing Alessi to be one of the protagonists of the Italian Design Factories phenomenon. When I think about Alessi's innovative ideas, I refer to Alberto Alessi's entrepreneurial vision in the early 1970s. Back then, Alberto decided to make a significant change to the direction of the family business by starting to collaborate with external architects and designers. This decision revolutionized the development of new products and redefined Alessi's brand identity. Alberto's vision was based on profound ideas that now underpin design. Briefly, design means overcoming the typical concept of mass production with respect to functional products. Instead, the industry can be stimulated by the power of human creativity to produce small works of democratic art that deepen our daily experience of the world. This choice, which today may appear "normal," at the time, led to a substantial paradigm shift for Alessi, as the industry went from being a traditional quality household industry, to being a laboratory of experimentation in the field of applied arts. Thanks to this philosophical approach, Alessi has become a cultural mediator between the best expressions of creativity on the one hand and the wishes and dreams of the public on the other. Alberto defines his role in the title of his book *The Dream Factory*,[1] suggesting that dreams are key to innovation because one of our missions is to match the need, not always conscious but inherent in each person, for art and poetry. By virtue of this vision, it is clear that Alessi's role in a consumer society is to create products that are able to reconcile the unpredictable, challenging, and innovative imagination of designers and the competitive and changing market rules. I prefer not to use the term "consumer" when I talk about our customers, because our products shouldn't be purchased to be consumed; they should be lived and participated in with the same intensity with which we attend a theatrical show.

We consider our products as small works of art, and this is confirmed by the over 50 contemporary art museums that house our products in their collections. Therefore, instead of the term consumer, I prefer that of "public," because the objects we produce are presences that inhabit and animate the domestic landscape, enriching our lives with happiness and beauty.

Tackling the world market through an artistic interpretation of the industry was the great innovative idea that underlies Alessi, but it is not enough to call good designers "innovators." The real secret of Alessi's innovation lies in the cultural vision that sustains the whole ecosystem, in the values that are attributed to the relationship between people, to the product and to the ways in which it is conceived, developed, and communicated. A central but fragile part of my role as a Design Manager is the mediation between the various actors who collaborate on our projects. Conflicting goals are everywhere in the product development process, because the desires of the designers, the constraints of the technicians, the needs of the salespeople, and the timing of the production often follow divergent, sometimes opposite, trajectories. It is here, above all, that you can make a difference, because the practice of design is a team effort, and the key to a good result depends very much on the personal understanding created between the various actors sharing the challenge and on the mutual trust placed in the relationship between designer and company.

From this alchemy of elements, our innovative ideas are born, from the seriousness with which we face dreams and from the desire to offer a deeper and more engaging experience of everyday life.

Where do you find sources of inspiration for new ideas or opportunities?

The first source of inspiration is the designers. Throughout our history, we have collaborated with over 300 of the most important contemporary architects and designers, establishing beautiful human relationships that go beyond the mere professional relationship and that have led us to investigate, reformulate and bring together the society in which we live. In order to be able to propose innovative ideas to the market, we must, first of all, succeed in interpreting it – and a good interpretation represents a fertile ground for generating ideas that respond to needs, desires, and gaps in the market. Sometimes we say that our marketing agents are the designers. In fact, we place a lot of trust in the designers' creative sensitivity, and we often rely on their intuition to see the future and try to define new trends.

For these reasons and because of the artistic spirit that characterizes our work practice, at Alessi marketing has a particular role in acting as a lever at the service of the product rather than the opposite.

In reality, our approach to the development of new products follows a logic opposed to that of traditional marketing. We follow a somewhat reverse flow of development; that is, we start from the inspiration, from poetry. We trust the unique qualities of human sensitivity and believe that there is no marketing research that can provide us with the kind of input we seek. When we are convinced that we have identified a good "dream" to focus on, we descend (from the clouds) top-down towards the definition of the product, a path full of virtuous compromises. Through a delicate work of mediation between the various figures involved in the development process, we try to guarantee a result that represents the best possible balance between respect for the original idea, production constraints, and market rules. In a nutshell, we follow the path that in the 1940s the American designer Raymond Loewy defined as the MAYA Principle:[2] Most Advanced Yet Acceptable. In fact, we constantly try to explore new languages and avant-garde aesthetic solutions, but always with the aim of achieving an acceptable output from the market in terms of aesthetic appreciation, function, and price.

The very reason for the Italian Design Factories should not be to create exclusive objects that are comprehensible and accessible only to a small circle of experts, the so-called *design victims*. The real goal should be inclusive, should offer happiness to the general public, and should respond to the needs and desires of society with objects that can be loved by many. Our mission is to explore the infinite possibilities of human creativity via untold roads. This modus operandi was defined by Alberto Alessi as "the practice of borderline," the strategic essence of our work. The *borderline* is to be considered an enigmatic boundary line that separates the area of the possible, that is, what could become real (i.e., really desired objects, loved and possessed by the people) and the area of the impossible (i.e., objects too far from what people are ready to understand and desire).

This is the territory in which we define our practice, a difficult and risky practice, founded from passion and driven by the hope of being able to offer emotions that enrich our lives. In any case, the result, especially in commercial terms, is never guaranteed. The *borderline* is neither visible nor definable by market research. The only way to see it is to take risks, to stay as close as possible to that precipice, and to sometimes fall. The contribution that Alessi can make to consumer society is precisely this, to push the boundaries of the invisible line that separates the present from the future, to build new poetic experiences, and to give depth to the system of objects of which we are part.

When you or your team have identified new ideas, how do you select the ones to pursue and the ones to discard? Is there a set approach or methodology?

First of all I think it is important to communicate how new ideas are born at Alessi.

Basically, we have three ways to generate products. The first is designers coming to us with ideas. We receive more than a thousand proposals every year, and they can come from a huge variety of people in the design world, from recent graduates to famous names in the world of architecture. Designers know that we are always open to receiving challenging proposals, and we know that when they have unconventional projects in mind they think of us.

The second approach is from a marketing perspective, where we commission designers to interpret a given product. Here is another important part of my work, being able to identify the right combination between object and creative personality, between stimulus and response. This is also a gamble, and it doesn't always work out. However, the important thing is to put the creative person in a position where he or she can express himself or herself. For this reason, our briefings are never prescriptive with respect to the aesthetic aspects. We limit ourselves to framing the type of product that interests us. We contextualize it through a market analysis that defines the benchmarks and then list the minimum functional characteristics desired. Then, the designer is free to express his or her imagination, to follow his or her sensitivity, even going beyond our brief. It happens that the best ideas are born out of transgression, and we are always very interested in being surprised.

The third way is workshops. These are research sessions that we organize in collaboration with designers, universities, or other companies. These projects can last from a few days to a whole year and are opportunities for the highest experimental content; we consider these workshops as true laboratories for investigating contemporary aesthetics and technology.

Through these three approaches, we create the collection of new ideas and from here we open one of the most delicate and decisive phases, that is, the selection of projects to work on and invest resources in. In order to make these important decisions, in addition to relying on the sensitivity and culture of the product development team, Alberto Alessi has developed a mathematical model useful for evaluating the potential of a project proposal, the "Formula for Success."[3] This formula is applied in marketing tests and predicts the potential success of the products we're working on. The purpose of the formula is certainly not to understand what we think of the project we're dealing with – and much less what the designer who created it thinks – but to understand how the public might react if we decide to present it to the market. The test has four fundamental parameters: (F) function, (P) price, (CL) communication potential, and (SMI) ability to stimulate sensation-memory-imaginary. Function defines the degree of usability, ease, and convenience of use. Price is used to compare our proposal with the market offer on an economic level. Communication-language establishes whether an object is trendy, how much it is able to transmit culture and respond to people's self-representation; in other words, it responds to questions of "status" or "style." It assesses the potential of the relationship an object is able to establish between the owner and others who see the owner in possession of it. Finally, SMI, the most important parameter of any of Alessi's products, refers to a person's emotional and psychological sphere. It concerns the pleasure that the object generates to the senses, the impression it makes on one's memory and on the unconscious through the generation of emotions. It responds to the need for creativity and is an extremely subjective assessment that influences the purchase decision. For each of these parameters, a panel of individuals gives a score ranging from 1 to 5, where 1 is the minimum and 5 the maximum. The sum of the four parameters provides a final score ranging from 0 to 20. A score of more than 16 identifies a potential best seller, between 16 and 14 a successful product, between 14 and 12 an average product, between 12 and 10 a small series, and under 10 a flop. An important thing to keep in mind is that the formula of success is a tool built specifically for and on Alessi, so it is not possible to understand it as a universal method for the analysis of products. Another important aspect is that the formula is an instrument, very useful, but not sufficient for decision making. In other words, the result obtained in the marketing test doesn't automatically translate into the final choice; this is always the result of our interpretation of the information that emerges from the test. In fact, there may be cases in which a product has obtained a low final score for reasons related to price and functionality but has obtained excellent results on the parameters CL and

SMI; in cases like this, we might continue the development, albeit aware of the potential commercial failure but confident of the cultural impact in terms of aesthetic innovation.

This methodological approach allows us to determine the center of gravity of each new proposal and represents a compass to guide us in the immensity of what is possible from a creative point of view.

Do you have any beliefs about innovation that might not necessarily be held by others?

In my work at Alessi I live on the borderline, in a place that is all about innovation and the search for the "new" in every sense. I have learned that innovation is not a merely functionalist and linear concept. Innovation should not be measured solely according to the logic of maximizing performance or profit but also according to values that are more difficult to quantify but which are decisive for the quality of our life. Making innovation, trying to stay as close as possible to the borderline, means first of all to question one's own certainties, to reformulate the questions we ask ourselves and to open up to the unpredictability of the answers. In Alessi, we base our practice on innovation, which, however, is only sometimes related to improving a product's function – this is because it is difficult to find functional innovation margins in old typologies such as cutlery or a basket, while we believe that there is still ample room for exploration of the poetic relationship that we establish with objects and their aesthetic.

The mass production industry operates according to very different logics from those of the Italian Design Factories. Mass production tries to keep as far away from the borderline as possible to avoid risk and maximize results in terms of volume. In doing so, however, little by little, everyone produces the same smartphones, the same televisions and the same cars. In Italy, we say that there is no venture without risk, and the risk is inevitably connected to potential failure, but failure can be an extremely precious moment. Therefore, I believe that we should give more importance to the "flops" and capitalize on the awareness that is derived from failure. Flops are those projects which are located beyond the borderline and are not clearly identifiable with the "Formula for Success." These are challenging projects that we develop with love, but which in the market test fall into the area of the impossible. Despite the many resources invested and the passion involved in their development, the public does not understand them and does not accept them.

Paradoxically, these flops are a characteristic element of the Alessi practice, a precious resource that indeed is the only way to probe the real position of the borderline. And it is precisely at the moment of failure that one becomes aware of where the limit is. And this then guides future choices.

I believe that in order to be able to build an evolved vision of "progress," innovation should also be valued from a more critical point of view, a point of view of questioning and rediscovering the world we create.

Notes

1 See Alessi, A. (2016). *The Dream Factory: Alessi Since 1921*. Milan: Rizzoli.
2 The MAYA Principle is the secret behind several classics of industrial design, including the Coca-Cola bottle, the Shell Oil logo and the Greyhound logo. Loewy's secret was essentially to design for the future – but to deliver the future gradually. Loewy said that "The adult public's taste is not necessarily ready to accept the logical solutions to their requirements if the solution implies too vast a departure from what they have been conditioned into accepting as the norm." See https://www.raymond-loewy.com.
3 The Formula is also described in Verganti, R. (2009). *Design Driven Innovation: Changing the Rules of Competition by Radically Innovating What Things Mean*. Boston, MA: Harvard Business Press, pp. 183–184.

7

CÉLINE LE COTONNEC

Keep in mind innovation is neither only about tech, nor only about start-ups. Everything can be innovative.

Céline Le Cotonnec is Chief Data Officer for AXA Singapore. Handling business intelligence, big data/analytics and innovation, she leads data management, transformation and reporting teams, as well as running big data projects and setting up partnerships with (FinTech) start-ups and other data companies.

Prior to AXA, Céline was Head of Connected Services, Digital and Mobility for PSA Peugeot Citroen Asian Direction in Shanghai where her mission was to define an innovative user experience while developing new business models using connected cars data. Working closely with R&D, open innovation teams and external partners from automotive to other disruptive industries, her goal was to manage effective coordination within PSA Joint Ventures across the three brands Peugeot, Citroen, and DS.

In 2008, while she was working as Business Development Manager in the Automotive and New Technology Department of the Economic French Trade Commission in Shanghai, Céline founded Shanghai Young Bakers, an innovative charity program providing one-year fully sponsored training to underprivileged Chinese youth.

What is innovation to you?

I think the first really innovative project that I worked on was an NGO that I set up in China, called Shanghai Young Bakers. We set up a training program for underprivileged Chinese youth to study French bakery, with the aim of empowering them so they could find better jobs. For the program to succeed we had to take an innovative approach, to do things differently from previous NGO attempts to help the underprivileged.

First, Shanghai Young Bakers is not a regular NGO. We started by asking other NGOs working with the underprivileged in China about the problems they face. They told us that most NGOs provide education for free, but prospective participants cannot afford not to work while undertaking study. Once these kids reach the age of 12 or 13, they are usually told, "Okay, you have two hands, two feet. You are eating every day. So now go and find a job." That is how these kids end up in factories or in the fields. Even though they have the capacity and willingness to keep studying, they can't afford it.

Second, we approached the problem from an economic perspective. Where is there a skills gap in China? Where could we find opportunity for those kids to get a second chance in life? Since we [the founders] are French, we were interested in the sort of bread we ate at home, which was not widely available in China. In 2005, bakeries were emerging, such as Paul and Carrefour, but these bakers also faced a major problem: there was no bakery training in China. So we identified an opportunity and went about setting up the program together with a team of volunteers.

While there are many similar projects, we were initially inspired by a baking center set up in an orphanage in Vietnam called "Les Enfants de Hué" by two French guys. We wanted to do something similar. However, differences in licensing and food regulations between Shanghai and Vietnam meant we could not really apply the same model. So we developed our own specific professional training program. We drew inspiration from the French curriculum where students work part-time and study part-time [apprenticeships], which did not exist in China. For the program to work, it was absolutely crucial that the bakeries or hotels paid the students, because otherwise they would not be able to take part.[1]

For the project to succeed, we needed all the competing bakery outlets to become partners. Getting these competitors to work together is one of the most innovative aspects of this project. We gathered all the competitors – those opening bakeries and all the five-star hotels around Shanghai – around the table and said, "We have the same problem. Let's try to achieve a common goal of training bakers, while working together to do good, by training orphans and giving them a second chance."

A lot of people told us that this would not work, particularly when it comes to making competitors collaborate. After all, a skilled baker is also a competitive advantage for his or her employer. But through perseverance and some strategic decision making regarding the legal and financial structure, the project finally began and has now been running for ten years.

A key innovative aspect of this approach is that it's sustainable. This sets it apart from other NGO programs – giving students access to education is only part of the solution. In our program the students are paid so they can support their families. The bakeries and hotels gain skilled employees. Central to our philosophy is that the students don't just learn about baking; they learn about solidarity. They learn that the program is not actually free – they must pay back to society by helping others. So they are expected to be involved in volunteering, to help others as they have been helped. For example, they go to rural areas in China to help other NGOs as volunteers. This empowers them to believe that they can change things for the better.

Today, we can see that some of the rural kids or kids formerly living on the street or in poverty are now chefs or bakers in five-star hotels in China. This program helped them to turn around their lives. It's an example of social innovation in action.

As the program has developed, we have considered other ways of innovating. Now that this social enterprise is 23% self-financed, we have been asked why we don't set up a fee-paying training school open to everyone. However, we don't want to reduce the job market for our underprivileged kids when they graduate.

Others ask, "Why don't you sell the bread that you make during the training?" In fact, we kind of do that through our "solidarity baskets." People can subscribe to receive bread on a weekly basis. But at the same time, we do not want to become a competitor to our partners. So this has always been a very tight balance between charity and self-sufficiency.

Our goal is to reach 50% self-financing for the program by developing our catering activities and basic training courses (that don't lead to certification). If we are able to get more funds, we could open another training program may be dedicated to a specific group of people, for example, the blind.

Turning to another example of innovation, this one from the corporate world when I worked at Groupe PSA. I was hired by PSA to set up the purchasing department, and the way I helped create this department was innovative.

Usually, a buyer in the purchasing or procurement department in a big organization, especially a car manufacturer, is focused on the cheaper, the better. But I was in charge of buying services, such as R&D services, media, digital, events, agencies. And when you are buying creativity, you cannot really buy the cheapest because you will not be able to sell cars if the media space or the launch event aren't good.

So we implemented different metrics that made it possible for our partner to share in the success. By collaborating with internal clients like marketing, or R&D, they had a stake in the success of the project and could get a bonus at the end or a penalty if things didn't work out.

This was also a way to expand our supplier panel. Because in China, PSA is not the dominant car manufacturer, unlike in France. An automotive event agency that wants to work in France has two choices: Renault or PSA. In China there are hundreds of car manufacturers so if you want to get the best agencies for your launch event or during the auto show, you need to create a special relationship with your supplier. It is not only about price. It is really about setting up a mutually strategic partnership.

I do not see purchasing as buyers oppressing vendors. If it is all about price and your vendor is not making money, then the vendor will no longer be in business. Then you can't access the services you need. It's not sustainable.

In my role as purchasing manager, we set up strategic partnerships to not only get a good price but to have a common interest in the success of a project. Essentially we created a team consisting of the vendor and our people, and tried to adopt a long-term approach to develop a beneficial buyer–vendor relationship. Clearly, this relationship should not only be based on price but should also be supported with other metrics such as those relating to corporate social responsibility (CSR). This is important, particularly in China, where a potential first-time vendor will always give you a very good price to get access to the market. But in the end, this is not sustainable, because if they do not make a margin, they cannot survive, and because when the price appears too low, either they are not paying their people properly, or they are losing money.

So I had one rule: If the price that we received was too low based on our understanding of average labor costs in China, the vendor would get kicked out of the bidding process immediately. Frankly, this was something rather innovative for a purchasing manager in an automotive group. That is not the way we usually do things. I had some arguments with my boss at the time, but it worked out in the end.

How did you convince your boss? Did you use certain strategies?

You are always taking risks when you innovate. You are not doing the same thing as others. Your direct boss may not want to assume that level of risk. So I recommend simply taking full responsibility. "I am responsible. This is the risk that I take, and if anything goes wrong, it's my problem." If that doesn't help, you may need to go up the ladder and say, "Okay, this is what I am going to do. If you don't agree, then fire me. And if you think that I should proceed, then back me up and tell my boss to let me go ahead so I can do my job." If I have to, I go up the hierarchy to get the support of someone who supports my view that the role of the purchasing manager is to develop a healthy network of vendors and partners in which all of us can grow together in a sustainable fashion.

What is the one thing that you do regularly (e.g., daily, quarterly, annually) that has contributed to your success in spotting innovative ideas/ solutions?

I perform benchmarks a lot. I always try to get inspired by others. This includes benchmarking within my industry or with people with a similar position in other industries, such as fast-moving consumer goods, luxury industry, or consumer electronics. I want to see how they manage the consumer, what processes they use and how they organize themselves. Who is making the decisions? Where does the innovation fit in the organization? Do you really report to the right person for your new business model to be implemented, for example?[2]

I think that benchmarking is a way to learn from others and potentially also to find innovative ideas together. In fact, I believe that innovation nowadays comes from merging ecosystems.[3] So people or partnerships that you would have never thought about in the past may help create an innovative product.

At what point do you consider sharing your idea with others, including those in your organization? What kind of evidence or support do you seek before moving forward?

I always work with a mentor so I can bounce ideas off someone else. I need a mentor to be able to work, and this person does not necessarily need to be my direct boss. Ideally, it works best with your boss, and if he or she supports your initiative and innovative ideas, you can really discuss anything and learn from each other. But otherwise, I always recommend seeking some support from a mentor in your organization.

And at what stage do you choose to share ideas? At a very early stage, or when you have done some research yourself?

Usually, I first share ideas with my team. I am lucky that I have always had great teams to work with. First, we think about how to test the idea, if and how it could work, and decide what the Minimum Viable Product (MVP) could be.

I also tend to use tools and methodologies such as design thinking in order to adopt the right process in defining an MVP for an initiative. So I tend to share ideas immediately. First, we brainstorm a lot. Sometimes, we have thousands of ideas. Then, we try to refocus on what could be an MVP. What is technically feasible? What could be the plan? What budget would we need? That is how we create a project so it can be financed and we can launch a pilot.

For example, we are working on a new value proposition for a new type of connected insurance that has never been done before. We are partnering with IoT providers in a new way. We thought a lot about the value chain and what is relevant to both parties. Because a partnership cannot work if it is only one-way; there has to be a win–win, just like in the Shanghai Young Bakers example.

Businesses need to be innovative but at the same time get things done today; that is, they have a portfolio of opportunities to invest in for both the short and the long term. How should a business balance the short-term necessities and the long-term goals? What has been your personal experience in approaching this particular challenge?

You always have various types of structures when you are talking about innovation. Do I have an innovative person in charge of innovation within my business and my entity? Or do I set up dedicated labs that are not directly related to the business, which might scale up and implement your pilot but risk the project because business is not involved? Or do I have a corporate lab come in and start working with the start-up in a certain way, and ultimately focus more on the short-term impact and benefit?

In the corporate world, I do not think that having the innovation function outsourced, or having a separate entity, is really the right model. Because then you do not have buy-in from the real business that is bringing in the money.[4]

The way we do it now – and the way I also used to do it in PSA – is to take both a long-term and short-term approach. Today I am in charge of data and innovation. So, for example, thinking about the long term, we have one guy who is doing all the scouting of start-ups and looking into how we could set up a proof of concept (POC). He also participates in all the FinTech and InsurTech events, and acts as the "Mr. Innovation" for us. So when start-ups want to reach out to us, they know that they can go through him and he will try to find the right contact within the organization to get the ball rolling.

But keep in mind innovation is neither only about tech, nor only about start-ups. Everything can be innovative. For example, thinking about more short-term goals, there is a lot of innovation in the HR space, too. How do you manage your employees? How do you make your workforce more agile and more connected? How do you adapt to millennials' expectations of what work should be like? So there is a lot of innovation happening everywhere, whether it is in your processes, the way you speak to your customer, or how you run your PR campaigns.

Within my team, I have data scientists working on data science projects, some of which are more aimed at the long haul. But I also have a part of the team that is dedicated to just doing simple automation; automating tasks like reporting, so we can show the business that we are also increasing efficiency and helping them on their short-term objectives.[5]

It is kind of a trade-off. I help you with this, you help me with that. You can't always ask the business to work on a start-up when they are already overloaded and can't meet their immediate objectives. You need to help and, at the same time, push. Developing a script for an automated report is not really innovative but it might save others a lot of time, and so they might be more open next time when I say, "Oh, I met these start-ups working on image recognition for a car accident in claims. I think it could be interesting in the long term to test this technology."[6]

You cannot do pure innovation [in big corporations]. Otherwise, you are an R&D center. And based on my experience in the automotive industry, even in R&D there is a lot more time spent on development than pure research.

In other words, if you were completely independent, you could exclusively focus on data science and cutting-edge technologies, instead of simply automating reports for certain other departments?

Yes, exactly. But because short-term goals are always of high importance – top line, bottom line, efficiency etc. – that is ultimately what counts. If you are only working on cutting-edge stuff but you cannot implement anything because the organization itself is not ready, you have nothing. You need to show that you understand the business. What is their business as usual? How can you help them? How can you support them and at the same time try to push for innovation?[7]

When you are in a separate, independent lab, you may be better positioned to catch trends. That may be fine for your global corporate strategy and for showcasing to investors that you understand that you are going to get disrupted and you are doing something about it. But apart from PR benefits, it is very difficult to implement from the outside anything meaningful within the core business and transform an organization, not least because true innovation also entails a transformation of people.[8]

How do you create an environment/culture that enables creativity and innovation?

I can only speak for my team because I can't change everything within the corporation. I encourage my team to go outside of the company, to see competitors, participate in events, and have discussions with others from the industry or outside the industry about how they are approaching different things.

However, I'm also aware that lots of people aren't really keen to do this, because they don't have time. From my perspective, it is a question of priority, and engaging with others externally is simply not always a priority for everybody. So we also do the reverse: outside-in. We organize inspirational talks by inviting an innovator from another company or another industry. Or we arrange some event on a subject of interest such as mobility.

For example, in the insurance business, some people don't yet understand that within a few decades, motor insurance will no longer be a product. Most vehicles will be autonomous and fleet insurance will be the norm. It is a different type of business model, potentially even a different type of distribution.[9] If you want to remain in business, you need to think about what type of product you can sell in five or ten years from now. The industry is changing, so we need to adapt as well.

At the group level, we have a dedicated foresight team. They share research on the future of work, drones, logistics, autonomous vehicles, and what the impact will be for us. This kind of bite-sized learning is often accompanied by impactful videos that tend to be quite effective in changing mindsets step-by-step.

What questions do you like to ask when someone presents you with a new idea?

The first and most critical question is "How do we make money out of it? What is the business model?" I see a lot of IoT start-ups approaching us by saying, "Oh, maybe you could buy my data and buy my bracelets so you could get data on your consumer and so on." So their business model is to sell me – the insurer – a device, which I am supposed to give away for free to my customers. But then the question is "Where do I make money if I do this?"

Assessing and managing risk is the core business of the insurance industry. People erroneously believe that by collecting data, I can reduce risk. In fact, collecting data helps me only to monitor risk. Reducing risk occurs through changing people's behavior. For example, consider connected cars: collecting the data from a telemetric device in a connected car is one thing, but making the driver drive better or more responsibly is a whole other topic.

We are often trying to push our products into the market without considering how we can be useful to our customer. We insure a lot of companies. Some of our customers could be potential customers to another of our customers. We need to see how we fit in this ecosystem, to connect these customers, and perhaps become part of this new revenue stream relationship ourselves. We still do not monetize all the assets we have.

To be clear, I am not talking about selling data or information. That, for me, is really an outdated way of seeing the digital world. What I am talking about is how we help others create a new value proposition. In the end, we are still at the top of our ecosystem. We are insuring everybody. So we have the possibility to help create value propositions for our customers and, perhaps, be the link in between. So this is where we really have potential for mutual benefit with our partners.

Right now, we are working on a data science project on retention, creating predictive models for retention of target customers that might leave us. This is particularly relevant for car insurance. For example, in Singapore, you are not permitted to have a car that is more than ten years old. We know who among our customers owns a car that is almost ten years old. We have partners, such as the biggest car dealer in Singapore, that exclusively sell our insurance products. Clearly, we cannot directly sell our leads to our partner, but there is potential to bundle an insurance offer with a test drive for our partner and then, provided that a person is going to buy a car, he or she will also likely buy our insurance because it is our exclusive dealer partnership.

People do not always monetize all of their assets, but they should. In the insurance industry, there are limitations, of course. Selling data is something we simply cannot do. But rather than seeing the problem, I try to see the opportunity.

Notes

1 Innovation does not happen in a vacuum. Analogous situations are often a source of inspiration, and a systematic approach to collecting and classifying these situations may provide companies with a powerful repository and source of competitive advantage at innovating.
2 This is a very interesting approach as benchmarking processes rather than tangible outcomes.
3 See also Peter Löfgren's interview.
4 For an analysis of the archetypes of companies' engagement with start-ups, see Weiblen, T., & Chesbrough, H. W. (2015). Engaging with start-ups to enhance corporate innovation. *California Management Review, 57*(2), 66–90.

5 This is a recurrent theme in our interviews: you need to explicitly balance short and long term in order to get innovation ideas and projects accepted.
6 Sometimes, to have an innovation project accepted, it's not about the value of the project itself but the (other) ongoing activities of the company.
7 This is a fascinating example of design thinking in action. You can come up with a brilliant idea that satisfies a customer need, but also you need to think in terms of your stakeholders as customers, and hence make sure your ideas fits their needs.
8 See Weiblen, T., & Chesbrough, H. W. (2015), op. cit.
9 This is an example of an innovative abductive hypothesis about the future of car insurance. A fully formed abductive hypothesis will inspire the rest of the organization to find ways to test it and further develop innovative products and business models. Innovative abductive hypotheses can be developed in steps. First, the new value proposition for the user is identified. Then, over time, a novel business model emerges. For a discussion about how this has happened in the case of Your. MD, an AI-driven healthtech start-up, see Garbuio, M., & Lin, N. (2019). Artificial Intelligence as a Growth Engine for Healthcare Start-ups: Emerging Business Models. *California Management Review*, 61(2), 59–83.

8

PETER LÖFGREN

Based on my experience, disruption is really happening in network boundaries, and it is important to help these networks find each other.

Peter Löfgren is the Managing Director of SynerLeap, an open arena powered by ABB aiming to shorten innovation cycles, and is also in charge of Strategic Collaboration & Business Development within R&D at ABB Sweden, a technology company which works with power grids, automation, and robotics. In both roles, Peter is actively searching for opportunities and synergies offered by different types of partnerships with both small and large companies.

With more than 20 years in technology and product development, Peter holds a number of patents and is a welcome addition to the boards of several start-up companies and regional research and development advisory boards.

To find out more about the work he does within the start-up ecosystem, visit www.SynerLeap.com or follow @SynerLeap on LinkedIn, Twitter, Instagram, and Facebook.

What is innovation to you?

At SynerLeap, which stands for "Synergies for Taking the Leap," we are inviting external start-ups into ABB environments. They sit openly and freely in ABB premises and can also use the infrastructure, such as the world-class labs.[1]

Based on my experience, disruption is really happening in network boundaries, and it is important to help these networks find each other.

One example of an innovative idea is a company's development of a real-time algorithm for checking what is going on in the stock market both in real time and retrospectively. They had an idea about new ways of programming robots. They had no experience whatsoever in robots before. But we let them use our space. So what actually turned out was exactly what they had intended: programming a robot in a completely new way using augmented reality.

As long as the industry remains very closed and we do everything ourselves, this type of innovation would never happen. This is just one innovative idea we have seen flourish in our environment. There are many more.[2]

For instance, we have a company that is working with athletes, including Jamaican Olympic runners. For training, they do not use traditional weights. Instead, they use motors as resistance for training muscles as you are running. Likewise, a motor may be dragging the person who is running, so you get used to running faster.

The synergy with ABB is that we are working both with motors and robots, while the start-up's exercise equipment is related to both robotics and to motors, so bringing this type of network together is a really exciting way to accelerate innovation. Sometimes it generates completely new, disruptive solutions. Sometimes it is just helping these ideas to fail fast. Either way, you share a lot of experience, and a lot of value is generated within the ecosystem that we create.

Do you have any beliefs about innovation that might not necessarily be held by others?

Yes and no. Our focus is really on speed and value creation. These are the most important things for us.

Since we consist of many kinds of organizations and partners, SynerLeap's direction can sometimes vary when you look at the different organizations' KPIs, and what we are doing here is trying to avoid that particular organization's KPIs. Because they can differ a lot between ABB and the start-ups but also our partners, including the city of Västerås, the county of Västmanland, and the Swedish innovation agency. Therefore, we focus on speed. Instead of talking, we operate by trying things out.

In fact, we see ourselves as the dance floor for these partners, and we want to see as much dance as possible. Sometimes, of course, failing faster is a result. But we always focus on speed.

So first of all, we accelerate the companies that come here. That is how the magic starts. If the companies are not showing up, we cannot really achieve much. So in a way, I think focusing on individual KPIs is a big risk. It can actually kill whatever is going on. To be more specific: what we would like to happen is innovation in our tech ecosystem. Who becomes the most successful actor in our ecosystem is not the most important thing. Sometimes it might be a start-up. Sometimes it might be the city, or it might be the corporation. But as long as it is happening in our ecosystem, we are fine with it, as that is our ideal scenario. The alternative is that we are too slow and innovation happens somewhere else. Maybe we do not realize immediately, but we would slowly become losers in our ecosystem. So therefore the first alternative – innovation within our ecosystem – is always better.

And the difficult part here is that you need to release the hand brake from whatever part you fit into in the ecosystem. Of course, everyone would like to keep control and to minimize risk. With that culture, nothing tends to happen or things happen just very slowly. So when you try to minimize risks what you actually do is you force yourself or the ecosystem to stand still. In turn, you actually end up increasing your risks, because standing still is the path to slowly accepting your own downfall.

That is why we choose not to focus so much on our own organizational KPIs, because we might not pursue certain opportunities due to perceived risk. We might not know what exactly will happen or who will be the winner. Hence, speed and value creation are of the essence. If we, in a fast way, can realize that we can generate value, then we should do so. Only then will we have a fair chance to have innovation happen in our ecosystem, which is good for every-body involved. In the end, of course, you can always draw the line: What is the ecosystem? It doesn't really matter whether it's a small ecosystem or a large eco-system. We would always like to be part of it, and not be excluded.

But let me be clear: innovation is all very positive, but it can also hurt. In some ways, actually, you disrupt yourself by opening up. You are letting others in that may be able to do what you are doing yourself but in a much better way. You have to understand that if you do not let them in and disrupt yourself, it will become worse for you. If you do not let innovation in, it will happen somewhere else.

Businesses need to be innovative but at the same time get things done today; that is, they have a portfolio of opportunities to invest in for both the short and the long term. How should a business balance the short-term necessities and the long-term goals? What has been your personal experience in approaching this particular challenge?

It is not a question just about the long and the short term. It is rather about us having a culture which makes us want to do everything ourselves. In looking at start-ups, we know what they are good at. They are fast. They are determined that they can achieve.

From a corporate perspective, on the other hand, you have so many people and you have so much combined experience and education there, too. Most of what start-ups do, in one way or another, you can do in a corporation as well. And that is the conclusion that has been drawn very often. Of course, that conclusion can be true. But usually things take much more time in a corporation. They might need to build on a certain legacy, so it might not be as future-proof as they might want.

From my point of view, this perception needs to change. We need to realize that we cannot and should not do everything ourselves. Considering the innova-tion happening in our ecosystem, it is actually better to take the opportunity to be fast and create great solutions within our ecosystem.

Regarding a balanced portfolio, that is, whether something is a long-term or short-term opportunity, I think that considering that is secondary. Above all, we need to realize that we need to be fast. It is in the interest of everyone. We secure our own future by opening up and letting speed be much more important than trying to minimize risk and keeping everything inside the corporation.

What is the most important thing(s) that organizations need to change in order to be more open to new ideas or approaches?

When you try to have collaboration happening, you have to have a kind of perfect match in between a start-up and the industrial lead in the corporation. At times, there is a huge lack of trust. But changing this is key. That is also why we have let the companies inside the fences of ABB so they can work freely and potentially walk into ABB offices.

But it is also the other way around: ABB employees could walk into the start-up's offices. So we have placed this growth hub SynerLeap in the middle of the largest R&D center in global ABB. This enables frequent interaction – we can drink coffee together and we can challenge each other. We can talk about everything that is not confidential. To me, this is very important in order to gain trust, and you can see the other party is actually investing very seriously in the relationship because they really would like to change the future and provide the market with better solutions. Likewise, start-ups can see that the corporation is not seeking to steal ideas or solutions but needs to be faster and have the newest technology, and, of course, is ready to do this together with corporate start-ups. It takes some time to build this level of trust. Meeting each other helps a great deal.

We also see this in the environment we have created. Whereas it took a lot of (manual) work to form a partnership or a collaboration in the past, today this can be achieved much faster. Overall, we are seeing greater and more quickly established collaborations than before when I worked on this as a Head of Strategic Collaboration and Business Development for ABB R&D.

So trust is the most important thing to establish. If you are not serious about working with start-ups, of course, you will gain no trust at all. If you are just there to maximize the corporation's benefits, it will be very hard. Instead, if you engage with start-ups because you think you can be successful together and you can help accelerate the start-up, it will be significantly easier.

For us, that is the route forward. We cannot be successful with just one partner. We bring together a whole ecosystem to be successful. That is how we work. Of course, one party may be a little bit more successful than others. But we win together, and we lose together.

But aren't you concerned about start-ups taking advantage of your ecosystem before joining forces with your competitors?

No. This can happen – absolutely. We have to acknowledge that. But if you are not trying to open up and work with others and build trust, then you risk standing still. You need to compare two alternative scenarios: by opening up, you are not in control in the traditional way. If you stay closed, you do not get the innovation under your "skin" either.

Once you build trust in this environment, I think the chances for a start-up to go to a competitor are reduced.

In the past, you could do business with a handshake. Now it is much more legal. I am not saying that the legal track is wrong. You should not be naïve. But we are living in a new age, and if you are slow, you will lose out. If you do not take any risk, there will be no benefit either.

Therefore, I strongly believe you need to be much more open nowadays. I am not saying you should completely change your business. What we do in SynerLeap is not the only way in which we work with start-ups. At ABB, we can be very, very picky on which collaboration, which start-ups, we invest in, so we need to work in different ways.

Here at SynerLeap we have decided to open up and make things happen. We have examples of other big corporates which have invested in the companies we have here in SynerLeap. Previously, you would have thought that was kind of stupid. After all, these are "our" start-ups. But they are not. We are an ecosystem. Thus, someone else investing in our start-ups is evidence that we are accelerating companies here, and we are gaining speed. It shows we are successful as an ecosystem.

And if my board says, "Peter, how could it happen that this other big corporation is investing before us?" I would say, "That is okay. At the moment, we have twenty companies. Just make sure that you do not miss the other 19." There are a lot of opportunities, and there are many players that can benefit from these opportunities.

When you or your team have identified new ideas, how do you select the ones to pursue and the ones to discard? Is there a set approach or methodology?

As an external company, you can enter our environment at different levels. We call it an engagement ladder. So if a company does not really know if their technology can be beneficial in the industrial setting but may be accelerated by being here in SynerLeap through access to industrial competence or the robotics lab, the prototyping lab, the high-voltage lab, and other facilities, we just bring them in on the lowest step. We then match them with ABB entities, and soon we figure out if there is a match between their solutions and the different industrial needs within ABB. ABB is a global company with 147,000 employees. There are a lot of needs, some of which may not be so obvious at first. Therefore, networking is very important.

If we see that there is potential for a great collaboration, we elevate them in the engagement ladder. This means that ABB may pay for a verification project or similar. A governance model controls this, so it is not a one-person decision.

We have someone responsible from each of our business divisions, from our venture side and our R&D side, to help make those decisions. I initiate it, and then we can climb the ladder toward business collaboration or investment from ABB. So it really is a step-by-step journey. If we realize after a certain period that there are actually no synergies, then the start-ups become alumni companies. They can still continue to work with ABB, of course, but in SynerLeap we do not have "stationary" companies. A couple of new companies come in each month, so we are trying to work with high speed and see how we can advance very quickly.

How do you encourage people around you to challenge themselves?

There are so many ways to accelerate companies and people who work professionally in that area. What we need in big corporations is to learn from them and to make sure they get in contact with the industry as well.

Many companies knock on the big corporations' doors hundreds of times and they are not let in. In the end, however, the big corporation might be completely disrupted. It is not like the start-ups aspire to run corporations into bankruptcy – not at all. They just have a passion for making a difference. Usually that requires joining forces.

Those who are trying to work against this trend, of course, become their enemies and often lose out in the end. You need to be on your toes and realize that if others are better, you need to stay ahead in some way yourself. That is the way forward!

Notes

1 Peter is discussing one of the approaches that corporates have to engage in with start-ups. In ABB's case, they use an approach that could be called "Outside In" innovation, wherein start-ups are invited to be part of a corporate environment where they can take advantage of expertise, networks, and channels to market and so on. The engagement with start-ups can involve equity or not, depending on the relative importance of strategic versus financial goals for the corporate partner. Similar approaches were adopted by Siemens TTB, AT&T Foundry, and Intel Wearables Accelerator. For more information about strategies to engage with start-ups and the examples above, see "Resources" in Part 3 and Weiblen, T., & Chesbrough, H. W. (2015). Engaging with start-ups to enhance corporate innovation. *California Management Review*, 57(2), 66–90.

2 For the importance of working with the network of your industry rather than focusing only on the technological and competitive development in your industry, see also: Hagel III, J., Brown, J. S., & Davison, L. (2012). *The Power of Pull: How Small Moves, Smartly Made, Can Set Big Things in Motion*. Philadelphia, PA: Basic Books. For approaches to set up processes for scouting the landscape and create hypotheses about the future, see Dong, A., Garbuio, M., & Lovallo, D. (2016). Generative sensing: A design perspective on the microfoundations of sensing capabilities. *California Management Review*, 58(4), 97–117.

9

JEANNE MARELL

You cannot just rely on users to unfold the complete story or to indicate what direction you should take. As an innovator, it's your main task to uncover unarticulated needs.

Jeanne Marell is an innovation leader with over 15 years of experience in-house, agency-side, and in the public sector. She has covered research, strategy, and all aspects of design: product, service, retail, and CMF (color, material, finishes). Jeanne uses her expertise from working for brands such as Bowers & Wilkins, General Motors, Hewlett Packard, Hyundai, Nokia, and Samsung to bring impactful design into the world of medical products. At Coloplast, she first led – as a consultant – the development of its "Design DNA." She then worked to roll out that DNA across innovation projects. In June 2015 she moved in-house, leading the team uncovering user needs, including implicit ones. Her team then ensures they are an integral part of the development of the next generation of products.

Coloplast has received numerous design awards, including RedDot, iF, and IDSA. In 2017, *Harvard Business Review* nominated then-Coloplast CEO Lars Rasmussen[1] as one of the Best Performing CEOs in the world.

What is innovation to you?

Different companies are at different levels of maturity when it comes to innovation. I've seen that during my career and during my journey with Coloplast.

Coloplast is a med-tech company that develops products and services that make life easier for people with very personal and private medical conditions. For example, we create ostomy bags to collect feces coming out of the stoma – an artificial outlet of the small intestine or bowel on the abdominal wall. We also make intermittent catheters people use to empty their bladder when they can no longer open up their sphincter muscle, due to a spinal cord injury as a result of an accident, a "side effect" or outcome of cancer, or a neurological issue arising in diseases such as multiple sclerosis. One thing that all catheter users have in common is that they will typically use our products 4–8 times per day for the rest of their lives. Coloplast is built on the ability to listen to users' needs – and respond with solutions that make their lives easier. We want people not to feel limited by their condition insofar as this is possible.

When you talk about innovation in this context, I would say real innovation would be changing the treatment. Sixty years ago it was a major innovation to come up with the first disposable adhesive ostomy bag, as the founders of Coloplast did. Since then, we have evolved that concept incrementally. We have made the product better and better, but after 60 years, the paradigm is still the same.

I first started working with Coloplast almost a decade ago while I was employed at a design consultancy[2] in London. Coloplast was a new client looking to establish a design manual as a way of cohering its massive portfolio of disparate-looking products, the result of growing the company across very different business areas. The products performed their clinical functions well, but due to the medical and intimate nature of the products, establishing a brand identity was challenging.

Immediately, as a designer, you start thinking that it's not only about making the products look like they come from the same company but also about how you can create a consistent user experience across the product portfolio. In our case, a lot of end users might not use more than one, or a few, products. But the healthcare practitioners who prescribe our products are exposed to many, and they teach end users how to use them.

When people are introduced to our products, they are typically very vulnerable. They might be recovering from an accident or a cancer diagnosis and surgery. They have a lot to come to terms with, and their mind is likely not focused on learning new routines. How can you create products that are very intuitive to use and don't add further negative feelings to their predicament? How can you design "away" the stigma and remove the feeling of illness associated with typical medical products that look sterile and alienating? What can we do to give people confidence? How can we make sure that they feel guided and secure in using the product? [3]

At the time, Coloplast's approach was to engineer solutions, not to design user experiences.[4] Our company's vision is to "Listen and Respond": we now strive to understand the full context of our users' lives, not just their medical condition; then we develop solutions that really meet their needs. This isn't a new pathway for Coloplast – it's how the company started, when the founder, Elise Sørensen, came up with the idea of the first disposable ostomy bag for her sister.

So we focused on design. That wasn't an easy journey because, in Denmark even more than anywhere else, everyone appreciates design and has a well-developed sense of aesthetics.[5] Everyone has opinions. To elevate design on the agenda, the company needed to have objective conversations around design and innovation. You can use these words almost interchangeably. The first thing we had to do was to give people the tools to have these conversations in a structured manner and to take away the styling elements and the reliance on personal preferences, such as "I prefer this color and that shape." We had to always maintain our focus on the lives of our end users.

Since then, we have been on a big journey. First, we delivered the Design DNA, which included a set of design principles, as well as guidance to shape form, graphics, color, material, and finishes in a way that is "Coloplast." And second, we delivered a vision of what future products could look like if we implemented this guidance. Now this was all done like a concept car – the concepts weren't engineered or cost-optimized. It was all about vision. But having a vision created excitement and alignment. And this was important to implement this direction across new product development.

If you look at innovation, there are many different areas where one can innovate. You can have technological innovations. That has always been Coloplast's strong core. You can look at new business models in our world. That is much more challenging because typically it is not the end user who pays for the product but the health insurer, whether that's privatized or governmental. Our end users only get access to our products through a prescription issued by a healthcare professional, so we have multiple gatekeepers. When we decided to also innovate on the user experience, our core belief was that a better experience for the end user would result in a higher quality of life and better compliance. This would then convince the payers to make our products accessible to the people who need them.

Has our innovation journey been an evolution or a revolution? One of Coloplast's bigger innovations from a user experience perspective is an apparently small change: that of the ostomy bags' color and material. When I looked at the ostomy market ten years ago, it was hard to distinguish between Coloplast products and those from its competitors. One of the first questions I asked was "Why are ostomy bags that 'pig skin' color?" It was because people wanted a "discreet bag." However, there seemed to be a clear, discriminatory bias in terms of the "skin color" chosen. And I couldn't help think that the artificial pink tone didn't really match anyone's skin tone anyway.

Meeting users revealed there is more nuance to the wish for discretion. It isn't about trying to make the bag "invisible" when naked. It is about hiding the bag when in public. Users tend to make very conscious choices about their clothing to hide their condition. Ensuring the bag doesn't show through a light-colored shirt means you give the user more freedom to dress as they like.

Having a "skin-tone" product created other challenges. There is a phenomenon called the "revulsion to the uncanny."[6] Imagine you're about to give somebody a handshake. As you're about to grab their hand, you realize it's not real. What do you do? It's likely you'll withdraw your hand in a reflex, creating a very awkward situation for you both. But if they had extended a high-tech prosthetic hand in titanium to you, you would've just shook it. No withdrawal reflex – you knew you'd be shaking a bionic hand. Everything that is not-quite-real is more freakish somehow. The same applies to a skin-tone ostomy bag. From afar, it might seem part of someone's body, but when nearby, it looks like an odd appendix that draws more attention.

So we changed the bag's color and material, away from the "pig-skin" nonwoven material. As doing a custom color for each user wouldn't be a viable business, we were looking for one color that best hid underneath clothing, regardless of the wearer's skin tone. We experimented with a lot of color swatches, putting them on people's skin and dressing them in low-quality shirts. We identified a shade of gray that hides well, universally. We then developed a woven textile in this color, soft to the touch, with a nice sheen that allowed clothes to easily slide over it. The material was more water-repellent too – good for showering and swimming – all in all really enhancing the perception of the bag. Initial responses were hesitant, resistant even, but then users tried it and found it worked. Alongside the innovations in the accompanying adhesive, this product family was a big innovation in our industry. We created a premium product experience, with a strong clinical performance and within the pricing constraints.[7] It really pushed the entire market forward.

When you or your team have identified new ideas, how do you select the ones to pursue and the ones to discard? Is there a set approach or methodology?

There are a lot of innovation models, in theory and practice. The one that I most often use in conversations, both within my user research team and with project teams, is IDEO's sweet spot of innovation.[8] It reminds us we can innovate in different areas: user desirability, business viability and technological feasibility.

When it comes to users, it's about understanding and responding to the articulated and observed needs and opportunities for improvement, whether practical or emotional. Sometimes there are challenges in the use of a product, and we can avoid those through different design. Other times, a product works well, and no one complains, but that doesn't mean we don't strive to create an even better experience.

Coming up with insights and a rational strategy on what we should do from a desirability point of view is relatively easy. Thinking again about IDEO's Venn diagram, though:[9] we are a business, not a charity. And we manufacture healthcare products that need to perform clinically. We are not only a user-driven company that can make decisions driven by our hearts and passion for people; we also need to find ways to manufacture and commercialize these desirable experiences.

What is the business case? We are not trying to convince you as an individual that you should buy our very nice phone, and that a small price premium is worth it from an experiential point of view. Instead, we need to convince the government or health insurance company that our product does the job and does it better than our competitors. And that is tricky. Most of these health insurance setups separate products in so-called reimbursement categories. For example, they're willing to pay $5 for a product providing a certain clinical outcome. The exact product choice is then up to the healthcare professionals (or end users), who only have access to products within the framework. Large hospitals or insurance bodies might work with tenders, too. Suddenly, there is no choice for the HCPs or users.

The IDEO Venn diagram – viability, feasibility, desirability – can explain a lot of things. It can explain why decisions are made that don't favor the best user experience. As a business, we need to find the sweet spot in the middle of the Venn diagram. A beautifully designed product is pointless if it doesn't reach the users because the business case didn't stack up, or because we couldn't mass-manufacture it at scale and speed.

Another innovation model I use a lot is the Double Diamond framework.[10] Traditionally, at Coloplast, it was very easy to be a single-diamond company: we identified a challenge, considered it a brief and immediately went into solution mode. More recently, we've been working hard on establishing the first diamond. We start by scoping the project: through exploratory research we identify user beliefs, attitudes, and behaviors. We map the current user journey, including situational needs and opportunities for improvement. We agree with our colleagues across the various teams in R&D and Marketing about what to focus on and make sure that our time and money are well spent in the second diamond.

Previously, in a single-diamond process, we might have misunderstood the problem, designing the wrong solutions. Or we didn't solve the root cause, but only a symptom. When we started looking at how we can speed up our innovation process, or our development process for that matter, we realized investing time up front to make sure we do the right thing from the get-go means we don't lose time in the overall journey.

Many companies enter solution mode without even realizing that there is so much more potential if you (re)define the problem. If you are a successful company – with success measured by turnover, profitability, etc. – then it often goes that "if it ain't broke, don't fix it." It takes a lot of guts to challenge something that works and invest to make it even better. It could easily be the case for Coloplast; we're doing well. We're a market leader, and our share price has soared over the last decade. What should we do differently, and why? Because we can help even more users.

Where do you find sources of inspiration for new ideas or opportunities?

Users give me a lot of inspiration, and they also provide us with a lot of feedback. To find out if your idea is good or not, you need to start by taking it back to users.

Never take their feedback at face value, though, and contextualize and synthesize it along with observations and other data points. Your insight will only be as robust as the research design and the team's skill. Users themselves don't hold the answers, but they can uncover lots of points for consideration.

When you have lots of ideas that users like and need to decide which to prioritize developing, go back to the Venn diagram. A very desirable concept without a business case is an idea that will never reach the users. Sometimes, of course, we do let these more aspirational ideas guide us, even though they, in themselves, don't make it.

The same applies to feasibility. If we can't make a product at the right price, speed, and quality, then it's never going to reach the users. Remember, though, that a perfectly feasible product with a great business case – on paper – that users reject won't sell either.

I can think of another example from my time at DesignworksUSA in California[11] when we were doing a project for Motorola. This was in the first few years of mobile phones for the masses. We were doing a very low-end phone targeted at blue-collar workers. Nokia had just come out with the first phone with exchangeable shells. Due to the competitive price point, we could only have an exchangeable front cover; the back had to be one color across the lineup. Our trend research concluded we should go with a lighter cool gray. I could see a shift in the color of TVs, VCRs, and CD players from black to silver. Silver wasn't an option for raw, unpainted plastic, but gray would look fresh and modern. In focus groups, users expressed a strong preference for a black back. The Motorola team felt more comfortable with a black housing too. This wasn't a surprise, people had "today" as a reference point, and at that point in time, that was black plastic for phones. A year and a half later, the phone was launched with its black housing. Meanwhile, Nokia was bringing out cheaper products with a gray back. Even more gadgets were silver. Nobody wanted black because it looked dated.

The message is that the average user of your products doesn't know what they are going to want by the time you're actually launching your product.

This is the magic that an innovation professional needs – and needs to convince their superiors of – to take the leap, to not just back the faster horse.[12]

Do you have any approaches now to avoid people saying "no" to innovative ideas? How would you help them to see the bigger picture and the trends?

That is always a challenge because when you work with executives in a large company, there's give and take between how much you can, or want to, serve up on a platter to them and how much they are ready to eat. You need to somehow identify a storyline that resonates with your audience. When working in user research and innovation, one of your key skills needs to be that of the storyteller. You need to bring people on the journey to make change happen.

Experience as a user researcher comes in handy here. You're already good at talking to people, making them open up about what is important to them. You're already very capable of empathizing with the situation of others. Use that same empathy to find the best way to present your ideas to your engineering colleagues, to your executive management. Create hooks that make them go, "Oh, interesting." Present objective data and show them the angles they hadn't considered or didn't fully understand yet.

There are lots of storytelling techniques, depending on what the content is, what outcome you want to achieve, and who the audience is. Sometimes you need to start with the vision, and sometimes you need to come with the data. Ideally, they're presented with some surprising or shocking, pertinent fact to which they respond, "We need to do something about this." Sometimes it is appealing to their own emotions and saying, "Imagine you're in this situation. How would you feel?" Depending on you and your audience, you can craft your story in different ways.

I'd also add that you need to have some maturity in an organization before you can introduce successful innovation. You need to assess where an organization is, in terms of mindsets, setup, and context. Then you can figure out what the next steps on the journey are because trying to go from zero to hero overnight is going to be impossible. It might be easy to sell, but it will be very hard to achieve. You need to be in it for the long run if you want to prove the value of design, particularly when working in industries with long lead times to get a product to market due to its complexity or due to clinical trials and regulatory approvals. Companies in sectors like healthcare and automotive can feel like oil tankers. They're very hard to change course. So don't try to do 180 degrees quickly. It's not going to work. Start with the low-hanging fruit and the smaller wins, and over time, redirect.

In my early days of working with Coloplast, the company wasn't as mature when it came to user research and design. We've grown tremendously. Stuff that we were fighting for ten years ago has become part of the standard operating procedure. But the journey doesn't stop, we can continue to push ourselves, move into directions where a decade ago, people would have said: "That's impossible."

Notes

1 Lars Rasmussen recently resigned from the CEO position and is now leading the Board. Kristian Villumsen is the new CEO, previously Executive Vice President of Sales & Marketing.
2 See Native, https://native.com/.
3 This is a great example of how to apply the SPICE (social, physical, identity, communication, and emotional needs) framework discussed in Fraser, H. M. (2012). *Design Works: How to Tackle Your Toughest Innovation Challenges Through Business Design*. Toronto: University of Toronto Press. Instead of looking at the pure function of the product and improving it, you look at the broader picture of a person's life and how she or he feels. Similarly, IDEO's design thinking approach may be helpful in this regard.
4 For a brief history of Coloplast, see https://www.coloplast.co.uk/about-us/.
5 Denmark has been a leading nation in the design field for decades. For an introduction to Danish culture, check out Kingsley, P. (2012). *How to Be Danish: A Journey to the Cultural Heart of Denmark*. New York, NY: Mable Arch Press.
6 In aesthetics, the "uncanny valley" hypothesis states that when a robot looks and moves almost, even if not exactly, like a human being, it causes a response of revulsion in the observer. A number of design principles have been developed to avoid the uncanny valley. See Mori, M., MacDorman, K. F., & Kageki, N. (2012). The uncanny valley [from the field]. *IEEE Robotics & Automation Magazine, 19*(2), 98–100.

7 Good design, as good innovation, is often about solving tensions and conflicts.

8 See https://www.ideou.com/pages/design-thinking.

9 See https://www.ideou.com/pages/design-thinking.

10 The Double Diamond design process model is well known among designers and was developed by the British Design Council in 2005. It suggests that the design process should follow four phases: discover, define, develop, and deliver. https://www.designcouncil.org.uk/news-opinion/design-process-what-double-diamond and https://www.designcouncil.org.uk/sites/default/files/asset/document/ElevenLessons_DeskResearchReport_0.pdf.

11 Designworks is the global creative consultancy offering services to foster innovation and business growth. It's part of the BMW Group and provides services in a variety of industries, products, and experiences.

12 See also the use of interpreters and Design-Driven Innovation in Verganti, R. (2009). *Design Driven Innovation: Changing the Rules of Competition by Radically Innovating What Things Mean.* Boston, MA: Harvard Business Press. Interpreters are good at predicting future needs and wants.

10

CHRISTINE NG

Selling an idea is a process, not a final meeting, not a final presentation. It is a process of how you arrive at the solution. The key is to involve the people who will benefit from it early on and make them part of the team in creating that perfect and remarkable solution.

Christine Ng is a Principal Engineer at General Mills who leads technology development in food ingredient and process systems to deliver innovative food product experiences to consumers. She received her PhD from MIT in Chemical Engineering with a specialization in Computing & Systems Engineering. As a trained system thinker with a broad technical and food science background, Christine helps teams achieve remarkable results by taking an outside view of the situation to understand how to play to win within the constraints of the business.

With over 20 years working in the field, she has successfully led and created diverse, innovative solutions that span all key food manufacturing platforms, product categories, food safety, and supply chains. Christine also leads long-term technical strategy development in new opportunity spaces. She formulates technical strategies to meet future consumer trends with demonstrated success in converting front-end innovations from concepts to tactics in order to deliver new and impactful business solutions. Outside of her work, Christine participates in expert discussion panels to provide insights on future-oriented technology topics and brainstorms with other cross-industry experts on issues at the intersection of business, consumers, and technologies.

What is innovation to you?

To put my thoughts in context, let me first explain my role within my company. I'm responsible for technology development. Within our department, we invent or figure out how to apply technologies to solve more unusual and challenging problems with the goal to drive growth and innovation. We're a bit like the think tank of the company.

To me, a truly innovative idea comes about when you clearly understand the situation. When people come to you and explain their problem in their words, it is important to not just take the problem statement as is. Usually, what you hear is the owner's perspectives on the situation. From my experience, to be truly innovative, you really must go deeper to gain empathy with the real issues being faced.

Very often, there is a hurdle, or a gap or obstacle, that you need to overcome with technology. Once you can visualize or articulate this hurdle, you'll realize that this is the place where you need to come up with a solution to overcome the problem in an existing product or create a new product. To gain empathy with the real issues, we need to get down to the people who are familiar with the situation at hand, interview them, and hear them out. That's how you can gain insights into the real issues that you have to resolve. Do not just rely on the story that you hear from one person. Talk to multiple people. The "Aha!" moment comes when you realize the nuances that prevent others from achieving the desired outcomes.

I think if we focus on technology to overcome what is limiting you from achieving the ideal result, you could create a remarkable solution. A remarkable solution is one that uses the minimum to achieve the maximum.

When you apply more than what you need, you end up having a solution that has been over-engineered, and in turn, it may come with a higher cost that may make your business less efficient. A remarkable solution is one when you have tightly identified what you need to overcome to get to your target outcome.

More importantly, in addition to understanding the physics and science behind the limitations, we also need to understand the psychology of the end users. In the case of General Mills, a product-based company, our end users are our consumers. Along the supply chain, there are also other people that you should consider as your stakeholders. We have our customers and then people who sell our products. There are people who must handle our products along the supply chain. Even though they may not be the end users, if there are issues that they must deal with while handling our products, they may decide they won't stock or sell our products.

Having a good understanding of why your stakeholders may prefer one product over another and developing insight along the way is key to understanding the problems that you need to solve to help a business grow.[1]

So ultimately it boils down to understanding what problems we need to solve. Once we know that, the solution could be right in front of our eyes. Just like Einstein, who said that if he had an hour to solve a problem he would spend 55 minutes defining the problem, and five minutes solving it. That is what problem solving is all about.

An invention refers to a new idea or something that has never been created before. Innovation refers to the "use" of an idea to create a benefit. So an "invention" without a use is not an "innovation." To deliver an innovation, you have to develop empathy for your users, which may include your consumers, customers, operators, and salespersons. You have to understand the choices that your users have, what options are out there. Essentially, you have to understand the competitive landscape. For example, if you are hoping to grow your business, you need to define why you are not able to sell more of your product. Once you understand that, you can identify your true limitations and search for a technology to overcome them. Once the problem is clearly articulated, you can go about solving it.

What is the one thing that you do regularly (e.g., daily, quarterly, annually) which has contributed to your success spotting innovative ideas/solutions?

I read extensively. I follow many bloggers on social media. I go way beyond my primary business, which is food. I read about topics adjacent to what I do for my work. I do that because I strongly believe that having a breadth of knowledge is the foundation for making connections – because you cannot really make connections and have that "Aha!" moment if there is nothing to connect with.

I spend at least an hour every night catching up on news and blogs that I follow and spend even more time on weekends. I go to Twitter and Facebook. Lately, I discovered that there are lots of great discussions and great ideas that people share on LinkedIn. I come across all kinds of wonderful things these days from my network. I appreciate all the new and interesting technologies and ideas that they share. Today, having a rich and diverse network is very important.

I read a lot of books too. It is great to have a Kindle as well as Kindle Unlimited because I have the luxury of just checking out a book to see what is in there. Not every book is worth reading. Because it does not cost me anything extra to look through a book, it is almost like going to a bookstore and flipping through the pages to see what is interesting. This allows me to go through a lot of information quickly, and if it is not very useful, I can return it and not waste my time.

In addition, I have access to many magazines through Kindle Unlimited. These are great avenues to get a sense of current trends. I like to check out magazines to find out what's hot in different segments of our society. Even looking at the advertisements can be very interesting and informative.

These are the primary ways I keep myself abreast of what is happening, expand my background knowledge. I actively scan what others are doing, especially companies that may compete with us.

How do you create an environment/culture that enables creativity and innovation?

Besides encouraging productive discourse, allowing people to disagree, I think it is important for a corporation to also develop a reward system that promotes creativity and innovation in line with their culture.

People tend to interact differently in different corporate cultures. In fact, even within the same company, a different department may have a different culture. To create a culture that promotes innovation or creativity, you need to understand the personalities of your team members and design a culture that would work for them.

So let us assume that we know the type of people we have in our company. There is always a particular kind of culture that would best foster innovation among each team. Once you have figured out what that culture needs to be, taking into consideration who makes up the team, we then figure out a way to help the team develop that culture.

To accomplish this, I think it would be mighty powerful to understand the reward system that is right for your team. From my point of view, it needs to be a reward system where people are encouraged and incentivized to help others, and people are incentivized to receive help from others. This type of culture promotes collaboration and the creation of synergies. What we want to avoid is creating isolated superstars.

Sometimes people do not want to receive help; they want to work by themselves. This trait could be quite common among highly trained scientists.

It is not that they think they're the only experts. Some people are just introverts and prefer to work by themselves. And when you try to team them up with somebody else, they resent having to spend extra time discussing their work with other people.

However, we all know that interaction with others helps generate creative ideas and sparks "Aha!" moments. One plus one is more than two. You need to incentivize people to give help, and receive help, and collaborate to foster this environment. What we want to develop is a culture that fosters collaboration rather than competition, and at the same time respects individual differences and everyone's need to have their own space. Great leaders must learn how to navigate and lead a productive team.

I think there is a lot of value to developing a better understanding of how you would give people rewards to stimulate a culture that promotes innovation, especially within the context of a large corporation.

In a small company, they often make just one product, which is usually strongly connected to the founder's vision. The founder of a small company tends to hire people who believe in their idea and have the right skill sets to fill in missing holes. In a small company, you have to believe in the company's vision, because it would be kind of hard to stay there otherwise. So everybody believes in the idea and works together to make it better.

In a larger company, on the other hand, there is a tendency to apply division of labor to achieve efficiency. Some employees could be several layers away from the company's senior leaders. People tend to work toward the idea that "If I do a good job, in return, I will get a good paycheck." It becomes more challenging to get the entire company to be involved in crafting and delivering the vision of the company. Given the sheer size, it becomes harder to get people to work collaboratively across the organization on a common goal. It is not uncommon in a large corporation to find teams working in silos. Even though they are working for the same company, people in a way may end up just working for themselves. In a large company, we rely on great leaders to help translate vision from the top to all layers and to eliminate the silos.

To be sure that we execute the right strategy for the company, we should develop a reward system that would promote the culture that we need to develop. Many people have argued that we should not *only* focus on financial incentives. Although there is some truth to that thinking, I would argue that we need to think about the whole package. Several factors motivate employees, and these include financial rewards, promotions, opportunities to work on great projects, opportunities to lead, and both hard and soft recognition of a job well done. All these factors, along with the personality of your team, should be taken into account when designing a culture that will promote innovation.

At what point do you consider sharing your idea with others, including those in your organization? What kind of evidence or support do you seek before moving forward?

Before I go too far, I'd like to first check with the subject matter experts. I'm a bit like "a jack of all trades" and "master of none." Although I may know many things and know many topics deep enough to start making unusual connections, I do not consider myself an expert in the field that I practice. For anything that I think I know enough to come up with a new theory or hypothesis, there is someone else who knows more about the subject than I do.

When I think I have come up with a great new idea, the first step is to go to people who should know more about my idea: experts who may be working on something similar or know every single product in that category. These very early discussions with the subject matter experts are extremely helpful, because they help you to either eliminate bad ideas or to refine the original idea to something better. Now the original idea may become a better version before you start telling more people. Sometimes, the subject matter expert may recount the history of promoting an idea similar to yours. They may tell you how they tried to sell that idea ten years ago, and what problems they encountered, or questions that people raised, or why they were never able to sell the same idea. This offers great insights, which can help you refine your proposal.

By not talking to subject matter experts, you are basically reinventing the wheel. Sometimes we do have to do a little bit of "reinventing the wheel," as the world might have changed. Although the wheel may have to be different, you'll be faster in coming up with the right wheel if you are familiar with past efforts.

When consulting with others, be mindful that everyone will bring their own bias to the issue. Bias is developed based on experience and background. There's nothing wrong with people projecting their own bias. That's exactly what experience brings to the table.[2] What we need to do is to learn how to recognize and filter out the biases and understand where they are coming from. We should always remind ourselves to be critical thinkers. It is always good to listen and ask questions, but do not just accept everything at face value.

Lastly, be sure to recognize your contributors. I always make sure I give credit to the people that help refine the idea from a raw idea to something much better. That's teamwork and again goes back to promoting a culture that fosters collaboration.

Think about the last time you pitched (or have been pitched) an innovative idea or solution. What worked well and what didn't?

I start with the value of the idea, not what the idea is. What is the value of it? What does it achieve? What does it enable you to do? Is this idea going to save money, or make more money? Can you sell more or eliminate operational problems to get people excited about the outcome? Once others are excited about the outcome, then you may go into more detail about how your idea can deliver the outcome desired. Then you can go into further detail.

We should think about "pitching an idea" as a process. I think it is much more important how you bring people along as you come up with the solution or idea.

Sometimes we identify some supposedly unsolvable problem. The problem is sent to the appropriate department, and then a high-caliber scientist will work on it independently to come up with a solution. Most of our solutions take three to five years to develop into a fruitful outcome. Along the way, there may be many choices about how to go forward. If you do not involve your stakeholders early on and bring them along with you – and make them feel that they are part of your team and make decisions with you – you may in the end find it hard to get support from them. That is just human nature. If you don't involve them in the early decision making, they may not feel they are part of the solution. They may not see why you rejected one approach over another. Even when you have developed a perfect solution, if you don't involve your key stakeholders along the way, they may not understand the reason for your choice.[3]

So to me, selling an idea is a process, not a final meeting, not a final presentation. It is a process of how you arrive at the solution. The key is to involve the people who will benefit from it early on and make them part of the team in creating that perfect and remarkable solution.

Notes

1 Too often we focus on the end user and forget that there are value-creation opportunities by looking at the other stakeholders within the value chain. A value chain analysis may go a long way, and low hanging fruits may appear unexpectedly.
2 We found this observation very interesting, especially given that one of us, Massimo, has spent part of his early career investigating executives' heuristics and biases and how to mitigate them. The truth is that there are some very good heuristics that make our decision making processes faster and more effective and some biases that

might give us the opportunity to see problems and solutions in interesting ways. For heuristics that make us smart, see for example, Gigerenzer, G. (2007). *Gut Feelings: The Intelligence of the Unconscious*. New York, NY: Penguin.

3 The added benefit of seeing pitching as a process is that you have the opportunity to refine your pitch along the way, and as Teixeira suggests, to pitch to the different audiences separately, using their own language during the pitch.

11

MARK NIERWETBERG

In business, innovation is finding a solution to a customer's problem or serving his or her needs easier and better. Very often, it is looking at the same facts and seeing new things. That's why I think, for innovative ideas to be created, you need what I call 'open spaces.'

Mark Nierwetberg is Senior Vice President, Transformation Office Technology & Innovation at Deutsche Telekom, where he has worked for over ten years. The Transformation Office strives to make positive internal changes for the company's Technology & Innovation Board area and supports other departments within their business and cultural transformation. Throughout his career, he has developed his expertise in business management, strategy, and communication. As a trained business journalist, he began working at Deutsche Telekom in corporate communication and later moved to positions in business management, including three years as member of the Supervisory Board of Hrvatski Telekom, the leading Croatian Telco operator.

What is innovation to you?

In business, innovation is finding a solution to a customer's problem or serving his or her needs more easily and better. Very often, it is looking at the same facts and seeing new things. That's why I think, for innovative ideas to be created, you need what I call "open spaces." Within Deutsche Telekom's Technology & Innovation, we have established a unit that is called Telekom Open Spaces. The name itself is kind of the concept. In the Open Space, we have three directions to explore new ideas. One direction is toward top management, one direction is toward outward companies, and one direction is toward employees.

The first direction is toward top management. We organize an event called 24 Hours to which we invite our top management and people from other companies or research institutions. Fields can go as broadly as robotics, cancer research, or blockchain. These fields do not have to immediately relate to our core business. Because we think of digitalization as a tool that will spread itself into various areas of our life, we try to explore broadly. Thanks to these talks, we gain more insights into these different areas of life and different areas of society or work. These speakers fertilize, so to speak, the brains of top executives and top management with the idea that having heard about the problems of one field, executives will be able to relate them to the challenges facing their own business.[1] Our aim is that these events could spark some ideas and give top management more insights into how other people are being innovative. I think it is important for top managers to understand that they aren't the only ones currently trying to crack the nut and that nuts can be cracked in different ways.

The second direction is going to other companies with a co-creation approach or what we call *unstructured encounters*.[2] So we have a small team within Telekom Open Spaces that is empowered to engage with other entities in a special way. They approach universities, researchers, start-ups, companies, and city governments in a non-sales environment.[3] Our team meets with them in a workshop kind of environment where the goal is to educate about digitalization. It's really meant to be like an exchange. And the idea is that we can tap into their problems and apply our knowledge and vice versa.

One idea that came out of these encounters, for instance, was an application to detect road damage with video analysis. We were running a workshop with the city government and presented our idea of digitalizing trash collection from private homes. The idea was that we could enhance the collection of trash by measuring how full a bin is using digital technologies, but within the discussions we found out that driving to a neighborhood on an individual plan doesn't work with human nature. If you were used to putting your trash bin out on a Thursday, you are not going to do it on a Wednesday just because an app tells you to do so.

Only through this somewhat unstructured conversation were we presented with the real problem: the city government has to check for road damage because of their liability as a public entity. If new road damage occurs which is severe, the city government should know about this within a couple of days because they have to assess if that is something they need to fix or if it can be left for later repair. During the conversation, the team at Deutsche Telekom found out that the city government has squads to check streets on a regular basis. The team came up with the idea that the city's trash collection trucks are going through these cities every other week, so why don't you put cameras on that and do a video analysis? And the administration people said, "Well, is that possible?" And we said, "Of course it's possible."

And it's a very good example of an unstructured exchange that led to a solution which is quite interesting for both sides – before the conversation, none of us could work on this because they did not know about the possibilities of digitizing this process, and we did not know about the problem.

We think that with digitalization of other spheres of work and society this will occur more often. There are people that have a problem, but they don't know how digital tools can help them. We do, so we need to work together. That kind of environment can only be created in what we call a co-creation workshop, where it's all about finding problems or matching problems and solutions and playing around, not trying to sell stuff.[4] Selling comes later.

Finally, the third direction is the program called UQBATE. It is a play on the words "you incubate." It's aimed at our employees and their ideas. Through this program, we offer employees a three-month scholarship where they can get off their regular job and follow their ideas. Just like most companies, we believe that we have experts of tremendous quality. However, if they are just tossing their idea into a mailbox, these ideas will go nowhere. First of all, those receiving the ideas might not be passionate. Second, without passionate people to support them, we lose those with potential. To overcome these barriers, we have given employees the opportunity to work for three months on generating and focusing on their ideas, and we support them with the resources needed to really pursue their idea.

Importantly, we see this process as not only key to generating ideas but an opportunity to teach our employees how to think entrepreneurially. So even after three months, if they have not succeeded with their idea, we still have people that come back and are energized because they know that in only three months they can do a minimum viable product (MVP) or a prototype because they were free of corporate processes. Of course, the corporate processes that we have also have a purpose, but in too many cases, especially around product development, they slow us down.

In addition to these three programs I just discussed, we also run a speaker series in the lobby of our building where we invite experts to talk about innovation or new technologies. These are open to people who just walk in.[5] These talks usually run late afternoon or late evening so people who pop down to grab a coffee also have the opportunity to listen.

We also run programs where we help managers to develop agile leadership styles. Note that we don't think that agile working is helpful for everyone, but we offer the opportunity to learn more about it from the resources that we have within our unit. We believe that real change isn't achieved by putting people into an externally run three-day workshop and then expecting them to adopt the new mindset by the time they come back. If we use an analogy, it is like stopping smoking. You can go for a week or two, but it is good if you have somebody on your side who keeps track of you and reminds you of your good intentions.

We started this journey about four years ago with several programs that were scattered around the company. With the establishment of the Transformation Office two years ago, we have put these programs together in a so-called Telekom Open Space unit. In terms of size of our unit, in the Telekom Open Spaces there are eight people in total, and in the whole Transformation Office, there are 40 people. The Transformation Office is horizontally layered, so it can work for any other businesses within Deutsche Telekom.

What is the most important thing(s) that organizations need to change in order to be more open to new ideas and approaches?

I do think that we, as corporations, need to get off the obsession of cost-efficiency in every area of the corporation. I do understand that corporations, depending on where they are regarding their balance sheet and their profits and losses, have to keep track of costs, as we aren't here just to promote the greater good. But if we say that innovation is at the core of the corporation, we need to pay more attention to it. We have to allow innovation to grow and develop.[6]

What I mean by this is this: as a manager, what we have to understand is that innovation occurs at the strangest places in our organizations. So it is not only your R&D department that will innovate, it is everywhere or, at least, it can be everywhere. It is fantastic when a knowledgeable employee all of a sudden comes up with an idea either to really innovate or improve a company's processes. But to create any kind of innovative thought in your company, you need to provide spaces and opportunities to foster innovative thinking. If we consider playing around and trying things out as a waste of time because it is not efficient, then we will not get there.

So, when you ask me what the most important thing that a company should change regarding innovation, I would answer: it is leadership attitude. Within the innovation process, leadership plays a very significant role. In a way, it is like raising children: if you do not let your children explore things or if you tell them to not do this and not do that, they will stop doing it. And this is exactly what happens in corporations. If your team leader puts up a 110% workload on your plate, then you do not have the time to play around. And if you play around and come up with something, and then they say, "Ah, nice, but this wasn't on your agreed term sheet," then people will stop doing it. With this attitude, big corporations are losing some of the best energy and best resources they have. And that is the real inefficiency! But it is hard to measure, and that's why managers can turn a blind eye to it.

So what to do and how to start? Well, sometimes we hire consultants to tell us what to do. Most of them just come in and say something like "We have experience in XYZ companies that are like yours, and we had the time to look at what works and what does not work." I recommend getting 10 or 15 people together from across the organization, and ask them what is wrong in the company or put a challenge to them, and ask what would they do about it. And then compare it to what the consulting company says. I don't think the gap will be that big. In fact, you have some people in your organization who are super knowledgeable. But most of the time, you do not allow them to play around. Instead we spend money on consultants because we are so busy.

Don't get me wrong – we also buy brain power from the outside. I am not saying that consultancies only come to the corporation with super easy stuff that isn't complex. But most of the time we are buying the time from the outside. If you have some of your brightest people and you give them a week or two off work, and you tell them, "Okay. Can you come up with a solution?" I bet they will come up with a solution. And this is what we should unlearn: We should unlearn to only look at efficiency measured in budgets.

We talk about "fail fast" and "new failure culture": "Yeah. We need to fail more. Tah, dah, dah, dah." And then we come to the office on Monday and we tell our people to work and not waste time, well, that's difficult, isn't it? There is this kind of trial and error that happens every day. And your workers and your team should engage in that, because that's when they come up with interesting solutions.

One example to illustrate this: We had a guy in a test facility who came up with a super easy solution to use the test facility virtually. Generally, the way it works is that the operator of a device or the manufacturer of a device comes into our facilities so that we can test how they work with our network and if we can optimize their solution. However, this includes traveling to Bonn, staying overnight, and so forth. In addition, it also makes you work slower because there are only so many test facilities you can have. This guy came up with a very easy idea to replicate this testing process virtually. Since we implemented it, we saved over €1 million. This all developed because a young employee spotted a problem and had been given some private time to think about how to solve it. He even came up with his own prototype. Imagine if we give our employees time to do this during their office hours. I think the potential of this is underestimated.

How do you create an environment/culture that enables creativity and innovation?

In my view, there are two main ingredients. The first one is that you have to find yourself a structure that allows for *open spaces*: some time off and somewhere you can play. The second one is that you have to strengthen the idea of bottom-up innovation. I do not know how this operates in international environments, but at least in Germany, I think that we have a pretty strong culture of people inventing stuff no matter where they are in the business and even if they are management or not. However, I have a feeling that more innovation power or the desire to come up with new ideas has been attributed to management or team leaders, and that is wrong.

Most of the time I would say it is the mix of experience and new ways of looking at old facts that create the most powerful solutions.[7] You can only find these mixtures in your best teams, developer teams, where you have senior managers and junior managers coming together. So you need to have an appreciation for new blood, diverse backgrounds, bottom-up initiatives, and for people just trying stuff.

This is what I meant regarding the leadership role. If you have executives and leaders who appreciate this, then they will say, "Oh. You four, you have a super idea. You know what? Do me a favor, invest like a day per week. Everyone else in the team will put up with this, we will manage! Next time if somebody else has an idea, you will give your time, and they can do it." It is give-and-take in the organization, but this requires managers with a willingness to create such processes.

The role of management is to create these structures. It has to be part of your leadership training. We should all have our executives trained to watch this, no matter if they are in finance, or in HR, or whatever. We need to train people as leaders who watch out for innovation coming from the bottom. If you have an environment that recognizes that innovation is a vital part of surviving as a company, rather than only sales and efficiency, then you will not kill this important part of innovation from the bottom up. This is why leadership training is so important.

There is one other side that is important. As corporations, we hire people on the basis of functions. We hire an accountant, a finance person, a technology person, and so on. But at the end of the day, they have to know the customer and the product extremely well. Because if they are not users of these products, they cannot understand how solutions can be improved, and they don't understand the messy process of innovation. That's why we have to train the whole organization to become innovation- and customer-driven.

What questions do you like to ask when someone presents you with a new idea?

For me, the centerpiece is always what customer problem you are solving and your observations about the customers. We are all smart enough – if you give us 100 of these Lego® bricks, we will build something. But if you give us 200 Lego® bricks, we will build something with 200. But that does not mean anything. At the end of the day, we are clever enough to use the resources we have to build something. But is it useful or can it be put to a use? That is a different question. Most organizations tend to look at their resources, their Lego® bricks, and just come up with something instead of looking at their customers and really indulging in the observation of a customer.

I would say the best ideas I see are from those who have really understood their customer. One of my team members would even go from family to family and watch television with them. He would bring some snacks and sodas and just join them. If you want to enhance your television product, this is what you should do. It is unlikely that a car manufacturer is best managed by passionate cyclists. That is why if somebody presents me with an idea, I ask them whether they have talked to 100 customers who have really given him or her the feedback that this idea is useful. These customers cannot be just your family and friends, as family and friends, as well as co-workers, are too polite to tell you your baby is ugly.

Finally, I have implemented a concept of *Desk-Driven Innovation* versus *Customer-Driven Innovation*. In my role, I try to make managers realize that there is a fundamental difference between these two types of innovation. In desk-driven innovation, you just look at your resources and what you could do with them. In customer-driven innovation, you go out and watch your customer. You cannot substitute looking at customers with looking at the results of customer panels. You have to understand that you cannot invent something at your desk and then throw it at customers, and then get feedback. From my experience, it is only when you engage in customer-driven innovation and you really go out of your office that you get very different results.

Notes

1 These events will facilitate analogical reasoning particularly between domain analogies.
2 Mark discusses the co-creation approach at https://www.telekom.com/en/company/management-unplugged/details/-making-cities-truly-smart-involves-more-than-just-connecting-data--504600.
3 The bible on open innovation is Chesbrough, H. W. (2006). *Open Innovation: The New Imperative for Creating and Profiting from Technology*. Boston, MA: Harvard Business Press.
4 This goes back to the concept of problem finding and problem solving and, for example, the Double Diamond framework (see "Resources" in Part 3). A useful reading is Beckman, S. L., & Barry, M. (2007). Innovation as a learning process: Embedding design thinking. *California Management Review, 50*(1), 25–56. Much more time should be spent on defining the right problem to solve in order to save time in the solution and implementation at the end. Of course, some problems are more difficult than others given their ambiguity, complexity, and the amount and type of stakeholders involved, like in healthcare, for example.
5 Serendipity has a powerful role in innovation to the point that people have talked about engineering serendipity. Lindsay, G. (2013, 5 April). Engineering serendipity, opinion. *New York Times*. Retrieved from https://www.nytimes.com/2013/04/07/opinion/sunday/engineering-serendipity.html.
6 This is a fundamental principle in the Three Horizon framework as well. See "Resources" in Part 3. Baghai, M., Coley, S., & White, D. (2000). *The Alchemy of Growth*. Reading, MA: Basic Books.
7 Compare to André Teixeira's interview.

12

TIM ROMERO

Everyone thinks innovation is invention, but it is not. It is invention plus execution. So it is actually bringing something into reality that causes people to change the way they do things, the way they spend their money; it is something that has some physical impact. And the second part, execution, is much harder.

Tim Romero is a Tokyo-based entrepreneur, author, and educator who has started several companies since moving to Japan more than 20 years ago. He is the host and founder of the well-known Disrupting Japan Podcast (https://www.disruptingjapan.com), a popular podcast about the Japanese start-up ecosystem and the first and largest of its kind with over 125 episodes so far. The podcast provides listeners with direct access to the thoughts and plans of Japan's most successful and creative start-up founders and has hosted both post-IPO CEOs and new founders. Additionally, Tim is Chief Technology Officer at TEPCO Ventures. TEPCO is Japan's largest electric utility holding company. TEPCO is also a founding member of strategic consortia related to energy innovation and research. Tim works to bring about change to TEPCO and change the way Japan thinks about energy. Tim also is a lecturer at the Shinagawa campus of the New York University School of Professional Studies, and is responsible for delivering lectures and managing course design and material development for courses focusing on entrepreneurship and corporate innovation. Tim has also started several companies in Japan.

Tim is internationally renowned for his creativity and ability to develop innovative solutions. His deep involvement in Japan's start-up community and work with enterprises and clients to develop new, scalable business models has seen him lead market entry for many firms. Tim's experience in both the Western and Asian start-up climates as an investor, founder, and mentor gives him significant insight into the technicalities of innovation and entrepreneurship. To learn more about his story, check out his website (https://www.disruptingjapan.com/tim).

What is innovation to you?

I think the best definition of innovation is that innovation is not invention. Everyone thinks innovation is invention, but it is not. It is invention plus execution. So it is actually bringing something into reality that causes people to change the way they do things, the way they spend their money; it is something that has some physical impact. And the second part, execution, is much harder.

Most people who talk about innovation talk either about the ideation or they simply look at people who have been successful and say, "Oh, tell me the story of your success," and they skip the implementation part. But implementation is actually the hard part, the part where ideas – innovative or not – succeed or fail. The question is always what you can do with the idea. It could be the marketplace. It could be the way processes are run inside your organization. It could be the way you are teaching children at your school … But it is the implementation part – the real-world change – that is difficult, whether there is a monetary value attached to it or not.

What is the one thing that you do regularly (e.g., daily, quarterly, annually) which has contributed to your success spotting innovative ideas/solutions?

You have to tailor what you do to your own strengths and weaknesses and be extremely optimistic. Any time I have an idea that I think is worthwhile and could be innovative, I try to poke holes in it. What is wrong with this? Why won't this work? Most of the time, the answer is obvious, often to do with cost.

However, taking a tailored approach means responses are different for different people. While I'm an optimist, other people are hypercritical of themselves, and they need to go the other way, rather than focusing, as I do, on poking holes.[1]

I have actually only done this once from beginning to end, but it is an exercise I recommend: if you are having trouble coming up with ideas, every day commit to writing down ten plausible ideas. These ideas don't have to be fully formed, but they can't be ridiculous either. So every day write ten plausible ideas, and do this for 100 days. When I did this exercise, it took me four months. You end up with something like 1,000 ideas, so two or three are likely to be pretty good.

I don't really go through a strict checklist to verify which ideas are good and which are not so good. Because I've been doing this so long, I can do this by intuition, based on experience. I guess it is mostly a creative process. Usually if you think an idea is reasonably good, the best thing to do is to get in front of potential users, whether it is customers or, in the case of education, teachers, and get their feedback.

How soon do you think it is a good idea to get feedback after you come up with an idea?

Immediately. As soon as the idea is kind of fully formed in your head, talk to people who might be impacted by it and let them tell you if it is a good or bad idea. Often, the reason innovations don't take hold is that you are missing a piece. For example, there is a legal obstacle or some reporting requirement that you didn't know about.

Another good thing is to look at who has tried to solve this problem before – and whether they succeeded or failed. It doesn't mean the idea was bad. Perhaps the execution was poor, or the law changed. Maybe the idea was adopted by a big company that is no longer powerful. Something that might have been a bad idea 20 years ago might be a great idea now. The most important thing is getting out of your own head and looking at the real world, whether that means searching Google to find other people who have tried to solve the problem, or talking to real people who are potential users. The longer you delay getting out of your head and into the real world, the higher your chance of failure.

It's important to remember that people fall in love with their ideas – and fall out of love with them, too. Just in the same way that you don't want to be overly optimistic and internally focused, you do not want to be overly critical and internally focused. So, if something seems reasonable, do not be afraid to go out, talk to people and get that feedback.[2]

Where do you find sources of inspiration for new ideas or opportunities?

I look for problems. So I ask myself, "What problems can be solved?" This applies more in the commercial and business settings in which I work. In these spaces you have to provide utility. In the consumer space, if you are trying to invent something or be innovative, you can simply be novel. Being novel is enough.

In Japan, everything is quite clear in terms of instructions. As a society, Japan is very concerned with protocol. When you interact with someone, there is a certain protocol depending on your relative social status within that situation. That makes innovation in Japanese a little less likely; it creates a certain rigidity. But there are also protocols for innovation; design thinking itself is a protocol. It is a pedagogy. It is a systematic approach, which lends itself to the Japanese context.

The US and Japan are perhaps extreme in that way. The US values innovation for innovation's sake. They value challenging authority to the point where, if someone is successful, they will go back and kind of rewrite their own story so that they have a rags to riches narrative. There are plenty of start-up stories where someone was just there at the right time with the right product, and went on to success, but the story always has to be tweaked to focus on their battle against the status quo.

How do you build a great narrative/story for a novel idea? Is there a formula?

There are lots of good formulas and they are all broken down into different types of storytelling.[3] I think that Dave McClure[4] and Dave Strong, the COO of IDEO, published really good pitch-decks. I don't think there is one right way, but there are lots of wrong ways.

The most common wrong way is just talking about your product or your idea, and not talking about the person or people you are talking to, their needs and how it helps them or how it fits into a bigger story. I don't think there is a specific way of presenting it. As long as somewhere in that presentation you are explaining why it is important to the listener and how the listener benefits or how the listener loses by not joining in.

What questions do you like to ask when someone presents you with a new idea?

It depends on what hat I am wearing. Over the last few months, I have been working with a lot of start-ups for TEPCO, and they are pitching, "Okay, we can do this, and bring this innovation and improve filling or transmission costs or hundreds of different things." I will usually say, "Okay. Walk me through a day-to-day example of how this works," because usually, they do not know. They do not know how the job is done now, and so they are in their own heads a bit. If I am looking for something more general, I will play the role of the potential user and say, "Okay. What is in it for me? Why am I using this?"

Consider this example. I've got a new recruiting app and I say, "All the large companies are going to want to be on it because it has got all this great talent from the universities." But clearly, you don't have talent because no one is on it yet. So why are they going to come on? It's how people respond to a question like this that separates the dreamers from those who can actually execute.

A good counterexample would be something like OpenTable. OpenTable was a standard two-sided marketplace. "We will have lots of restaurants that will be on this reservation system, so consumers will want to reserve through it, and we will have a lot of impact with consumers." But it worked the other way, too. They focused on building an app and said, "You can manage your restaurant reservations yourself, and you can use our service or not, and we will give you this app for free." They gained customers because they were providing value, and then once that started to build up, then they could go to the customer-facing side and say, "Hey, we've got all of these restaurants. Let's find out what's available in Tokyo right now." It's about thinking how you will get from zero to one.

Are there any principles, techniques, processes, or other things that might be good in theory but haven't worked in practice in your experience?

There is a certain amount of trendiness and fashion that goes through management consulting, and whenever the start-up cycle is high. Money legitimizes anything, whether it is start-ups, bitcoin, Lindsay Lohan, or Donald Trump. So when a start-up starts raising lots of money, everyone agrees we need to focus on it and be innovative and learn from this culture. It was like that even back in the 1980s, when there were all these conglomerates seeking to become more efficient.

A lot of people get paid a lot of money to be consultants to organizations and say, "Well, you need to change your corporate culture to be more innovative." It is a very safe thing to say because it will never happen. Everyone goes back from whatever presentation they saw maybe pumped up a little bit. But the fact is that you do not need to change a corporate culture to be innovative. In fact, even if you look at San Francisco, which is considered the most innovative place on the planet, maybe only 0.5% of the population is doing anything that is innovative. Everyone else is keeping lights on and making coffee and teaching kids and programming or selling enterprise software. They are just doing their job keeping society running. If you have a whole company or a whole society filled with innovators, it collapses completely. So the problem that most organizations face, whether we speak about countries or companies, is that there is no way for this innovative idea to bubble up and to be validated.

If a salesman in an organization says, "Hey, I've got this interesting idea that we might be able to break this product in two and sell it as two different products," then you, his boss, the sales manager, are going to tell him, "Look, you've got a quota to make this quarter. Go out and sell. Do your job." That's not wrong – after all, if the quota isn't hit, then the company goes under. However, there needs to be a way to go around the system so that this sales guy can bounce his idea off of someone in engineering that can actually make it happen. What San Francisco does really well is allow for these ideas to bubble up and attract capital and for like-minded people to meet.

I'm not saying there's nothing wrong with corporate culture, because there are all kinds of things wrong with it. But I am not one of these guys that stands up and says, "Oh, we need to change corporate culture to be innovative," because this statement is so broad as to be meaningless. I think you need to provide a way for innovative people to connect with each other and provide a path for that innovation to bubble up, and in all but the most toxic corporate cultures, you can make that happen.

How do you create an environment/culture that enables creativity and innovation?

There are many ways to do that well. In Japan, SoftBank has a yearly business plan competition. It funds a lot of the start-ups that participate, but even before the competition, there are people throwing emails back and forth and organizing meetups on their own time, of their own volition sometimes. DMM, a Japan-based electronic commerce and internet company that includes online shopping and video on demand services, is similar. If you have a crazy idea, you can pitch it to the President and he might say, "Okay, that sounds interesting. Here is a four-man team and you have an internal budget of half a million dollars. See what you can do with it."

However, in the accelerator space, there has been a real devaluation of the term mentor in the last 15 years or so. I think that someone who has domain knowledge can be an incredibly valuable mentor.[5] All of these energy start-ups I am talking to could have benefited greatly by talking to people early on who are doing the work they are trying to improve. But a lot of mentors now are doing it because they want to say they are a mentor, and a lot of the accelerators are trying to get the highest brand-named individual – it is just this weird dynamic going back to the "money validates everything" idea again. Accelerators are a mixed bag.

Do you think that the healthcare space is similar to the energy space in terms of adoption of innovation, such as blockchain technologies?

I think the biggest challenge in Japan is that the government controls so much of the healthcare space. So there is only one buyer. The Ministry of Health actually wants to be innovative. They have got innovation programs, but the government runs things slower. There are some pretty innovative health companies – start-ups – in Japan that are working with individual doctors, so it is possible. I've been unimpressed with the blockchain applications for health I've seen so far. The biggest challenge with healthcare is confidentiality of the data in that there are some instances where information like name and phone number must be disclosed by law. There are some instances where this information, by law, cannot be disclosed, and blockchain is just not good for that. In most applications I've seen, it is just not the right tool for solving the problem they are trying to solve. But in healthcare, in general, there is a huge opportunity for innovation.

Another thing that energy and healthcare have in common is they are both highly regulated industries, and that is a good thing. I would put insurance and banking in there as well, and it is frustrating for start-ups. They may say "Why don't we just try this and be disruptive and break things, move faster, break things." It does not work in healthcare, and it does not work in energy. I have been working at TEPCO for about a year now, and I have an amazing amount of respect for the power engineers and the people who keep the grid running. I think the modern power grid is the most complex machine that mankind has ever made, an absolute engineering marvel. When you think that every electron that gets pushed onto the grid has to be taken off at almost exactly the same time, and that you cannot really route power like you do phone calls or internet connection – it is just going to go to wherever the nearest load is – it's amazing. So the guys that are in transmission see all of these start-ups saying, "Oh, we have got self-balancing," and they say, "Yeah, sure you do. Sure you do." I respect their skepticism a lot, and it is the same thing with healthcare.

So there is a balance between regulation and innovation, and in cases where the potential for harm is really high, and where the potential for both short-term profits and long-term harm is high, those things need to be regulated. I now have a greater appreciation of why those regulations are good even though they do slow down innovation. And that is okay.

Notes

1 Mental simulation, very much related to mental time travel, appears crucial in the imagination of future scenarios and so the identification of possible new venture opportunities. For mental time travel, see Suddendorf, T., & Corballis, M. C. (1997). Mental time travel and the evolution of the human mind. *Genetic, Social, and General Psychology Monographs, 123*(2), 133–167. For the role of mental simulation in entrepreneurial opportunities, see Gaglio, C. M. (2004). The role of mental simulations and counterfactual thinking in the opportunity identification process. *Entrepreneurship Theory and Practice, 28*(6), 533–552; and Garbuio, M., Dong, A., Lin, N., Tschang, T., & Lovallo, D. (2018). Demystifying the genius of entrepreneurship: How design cognition can help create the next generation of entrepreneurs. *Academy of Management Learning & Education, 17*(1), 41–61.

2 It is often said that entrepreneurs and innovators have an internal rather than external locus of control.

3 For an excellent job in explaining different types of storytelling techniques to capture the audience attention in a new venture pitch, see Baehr, E., & Loomis, E. (2015). *Get Backed: Craft Your Story, Build the Perfect Pitch Deck, and Launch the Venture of Your Dreams.* Boston, MA: Harvard Business Review Press.

4 Dave McClure is most well-known for the foundation of the innovation incubator, 500 Startups, which was started in 2010. McClure's first project was the foundation of Asian Computing, which he later sold. As his interest in internet investing grew, he started to develop the idea for his most successful company, 500 Startups. His experiences have led him to become an expert in entrepreneurship and angel investing. When discussing his method of pitching ideas, McClure suggests that entrepreneurs first address a specific problem rather than beginning by creating a solution. His pitch deck guide is available at: https://app.slidebean.com/p/89nGI0EFxc/Your-Company-Name#1.

5 Mentorship in start-ups is a greatly underdeveloped but urgent area of research. Who are the most effective mentors? What is their background and experience? See Dowejko, M. K., & Chan, E. (2018). *What Do Startup Mentors Do? Founders' Perspective on Entrepreneurial Mentoring Functions.* Paper presented at the Academy of Management Proceedings; Feld, B. (2012). *Startup Communities: Building an Entrepreneurial Ecosystem in Your City.* New York, NY: John Wiley & Sons.

13

STEPHEN SIMPSON

I like to build things that are bigger than the sum of the parts. I really rely on creative understanding and creative insights, as they provide a road into the way things work, and then you take your chances that when they come along, they bring people together to answer questions that you need them to answer.

Professor Stephen Simpson established the Charles Perkins Centre (CPC) at the University of Sydney. Born in Australia, he completed his PhD at King's College London in 1982 and spent 22 years in Oxford, in Experimental Psychology, the Department of Zoology, and the University Museum of Natural History. He was awarded the Wigglesworth Medal of the Royal Entomological Society in 2011 and was made a Companion of the Order of Australia in 2015. He was elected a Fellow of the Royal Society in 2013 and is also a Fellow of the Australian Academy of Science.

As the current Academic Director of the CPC, he oversees more than 1,500 researchers, educators, and practitioners from a diverse range of fields, including science, philosophy, and engineering. The CPC was created to address the burden of chronic disease using principles from evolutionary biology and ecology. A major innovation of the CPC lies in its academic strategy, which was explicitly designed as a complex adaptive system. In any such system, there are interacting entities or agents, interactions among which lead to higher-order emergent phenomena. Such self-organized emergent outcomes cannot simply be predicted from the individual activities of each of the interacting agents. Similarly, the agents themselves cannot make those predictions, or even necessarily understand the entirety of what they are involved in. By bringing together multidisciplinary teams in a complex adaptive research ecosystem, Professor Simpson has found that interactions are leading to higher-order emergent phenomena.

What is innovation to you?

My personal practice of innovation has been informed by my biological training, particularly in regard to complex adaptive systems. This has not only shaped my practice as a biologist, but it has also shaped the institutional design that we have implemented at the CPC,[1] so there is a real continuity there. More specifically, my personal practice as a biologist has been to address large and challenging biological questions, as well as to develop a deep understanding of a study system from which we can start to generalize and innovate.

I am a biologist. In my original research as a PhD student and even earlier as an honors student, I had an interest in understanding locust biology. In our world today, there are a group of insects that impact the lives of one in ten people; these insects are called locusts. Locusts are, in every respect, a typical grasshopper. However, if you put them under high-population density, they shift their appearance and their behavior, and they become swarming. As a result, they can produce massive swarms that can invade huge areas of the planet and do terrible agricultural damage.

I started off being interested in locusts because they were, evidently, such a large problem. However, they were also a very tractable system for getting in a couple of essential questions about biology. How do animals know what to eat and when to eat it? How can the same animal be essentially two things packaged within the same genome, within the same body?

Over the first 20 years of my career, I had the opportunity to address these two questions in ways that required me to bring together disciplines that were traditionally separate. This initial opportunity is a very important feature of my journey as an innovator in the biological sciences.

I started with the question, "How do insects know what to eat, and when to eat it?" I began watching ten locusts for six days and six nights and recording every time they took a meal and defecated. This yielded a large body of data that allowed me to start thinking about why they were doing what they were doing, and when they were doing it. From here I started to develop new statistical techniques for looking at the analysis of that sort of patterning of behavior and data. I then started using that to define manipulative experiments where you could delve into the physiology of the animal to look for mechanisms which control feeding behavior. Ultimately, I discovered that the animals were able to respond to different nutrients in their environment; they would respond in a specific way. So, when the animal needed protein, or it needed carbohydrates, it would make appropriate choices in its feeding environment. Having done that, it gave the basis for a new way of thinking about nutrition, which was to basically treat nutritional biology as an n-dimensional hyperspace where animals require different nutrients and different mixtures to achieve particular outcomes like reproduction, or survival, or growth, or what have you. And that then became, if you like, a new technology for thinking about nutritional biology. As a result, with long-standing colleague David Raubenheimer and our students, postdocs, and collaborators, we developed these ideas and tested them. Then we started to apply them more and more broadly to human nutrition, human obesity, and the biology of aging. Some really big questions arose.

It was these lessons and that way of thinking about these problems that have actually revolutionized fields far distant from where I began looking at locusts in the lab. Ultimately, these lessons have allowed for a framework which is still visible in the way that we built the CPC.

From this, there is another key principle, serendipity. And I'll give you one example. When I was working on feeding behavior in locusts, I had built a reputation in that field. And then, in the late 1980s, there was a huge outbreak of locusts in North Africa which caused vast devastation to many areas. This corresponded with a worldwide ban on the major chemical control agent that was used to control locusts, a chemical called dieldrin. So at that point the world was faced with this huge outbreak of locusts and no way to chemically control them. As a result, through the United Nations Development Program, the United Nations sent a callout to scientists around the world that said, "We have money and we want to support new ways of thinking about locusts." As I was already working on locusts, I put a proposal forward about this biological feature that they possess. Locusts are non-swarming animals, but if you crowd them, they become swarming animals. If we can understand that, then we have the basis for all sorts of new ways of controlling them. For example, we could predict when they would outbreak and when they would become swarming. The thing that defines locusts is that if you crowd them they turn from solitary animals into a gregarious swarm. In my opinion, that is serendipitous.[2]

There was this big outbreak, they banned dieldrin, and I got the funds and started a program of research that quite literally allowed us to delve into the basic neurochemistry of that Jekyll and Hyde transformation. From here we also started asking questions such as "What does it mean in a group, if animals have flipped from that non-swarming to the swarming form?" and "How does that influence cohesive behavior at a group level?" And so, to start answering these questions, I needed to engage statistical physicists. Having done that, we were able to show that collective behavior emerges out of individuals interacting with one another. We were then able to start asking questions about the environmental circumstances. What are the environmental circumstances that will bring animals together to crowd them sufficiently to evoke this switch, therefore inducing a change in behavior? As a result, we had to work with geographers, and remote-sensing satellite experts, and GIS experts while we were delving into the molecular genetics of the process. From this we were able to bring together disciplines spanning neurochemistry through continental mass migration, biological control agents, and agencies that manage locusts in the field in Africa and Australia. In other words, we started with a small piece of biology and ended up with an enterprise that brought many disciplines together in a coherent way. So a similar sort of story to the one concerning nutrition. It was a simple beginning; we really had to understand the basic biology in detail, and then we had to take that where it led. Recruiting and expertise were required to answer the next question that became apparent, in addition to taking advantage of serendipitous occasions. If you are open to serendipitous occasions and seize them, things can happen.

Overall, this is my personal story. I like to build things that are bigger than the sum of the parts. I really rely on creative understanding and creative insights, as they provide a road into the way things work, and then you take your chances that when they come along, they bring people together to answer questions that you need them to answer. Individually, these people would not have the capacity, or necessarily the interest, in answering them alone. And the biggest piece of serendipity that has worked in that way was the opportunity to set up the CPC. That was serendipitous. It relied on a lady from Texas giving the University of Sydney a painting. I was asked to go to London with the Vice Chancellor to sell this painting, and while there, he encouraged me to put my name into the competition for the first directorship of the CPC. So, I did this and had to then come up with a model that would bring disciplines together to answer some big questions, solve some big societal issues, in this case, the burden of chronic disease – and I could see how to do that. The way in which, just as individual locust interacting with one another can lead to mass migration without any single locust having any knowledge beyond its local environment, you could see the same thing happening among academic researchers providing you set up a model where they could interact with one another in ways where their disciplinary credentials were protected and their expertise was valued. You needed an environment in which they could work with others to achieve something that they wanted to achieve. Then, if you built the system correctly, you could get impact and complex solutions to very complex problems for free.

And that's precisely how complex adaptive systems work. That is how the process of natural selection works. It is about gradually selecting alternative variants among many. This can lead to the evolution of incredible complexity quickly. It is the same set of principles that empower individual nerve cells in a brain to ultimately have conscious thoughts without any nerve cell knowing anything about anything else, or cells within a developing embryo giving rise to a newborn child that works perfectly without any cell knowing anything beyond its local environment. You cannot have a blueprint for this. You have a set of processes that you set free to come up with complex outcomes. You cannot prefigure them in advance. You cannot set KPIs five years in advance. You cannot strategize getting to a particular end point, because if you do that you kill the thing that makes it creative and innovative. You have got to set up the rules of interaction and the structure of the system and then you let it go and you guide it rather than manage it inflexibly toward a particular outcome. So that's it.

So in my view, you need to have a common mission but not prefigure how any individual participant is going to contribute to that mission. You just have to keep their eyes in that direction and see what happens. And things just happen that you cannot predict. You need to be able to have a system which captures those insights as they emerge within the system.

Do you have any beliefs about innovation that might not necessarily be held by others?

KPIs are probably now part of an old-fashioned corporate model.[3] Universities worldwide have adopted and adhered to this old corporate model of strategic planning long into the future, setting benchmarks and KPIs, and so on. The risk with that is, if you prefigure how you're going to get somewhere, you have crystallized the system. Therefore, as a result of that, you end up managing underperformance instead of celebrating innovation. That is a deeply dispiriting environment where all you ever do is manage underperformance. It's much more enjoyable to celebrate success. This sense of celebration raises expectations. It also brings people together in a shared vision much more effectively than essentially threatening them that unless they get certain numbers of metric points bad consequences will ensue. A system such as this just shows them how they have failed. We're at a time where money for grants is in such short supply. It's harder and harder for people to sustain what they're doing. It's better to think about ways of having people collaborate more effectively than to watch them starve to death through want of resources, especially when resources are harder and harder to get. Therefore, just like any starving population, they will become fractious and cannibalistic rather than mutually supportive and collaborative.

So it might be even more important in dynamic environments, if you have set measures of success up front, you might end up having to change them.

That is absolutely right. This is where the analogy of biology is so important. Evolution manages adaption in a changing environment. That is what we are all doing. At this moment, in a rapidly changing environment in all sorts of ways, technologically, financially, and in terms of the sheer advancement of the disciplines, you need to be much more adept and mobile. Academics, in my opinion, are already predisposed to do that, which is how we are. We are willing to consider different ways of thinking and are always looking out for ways to connect disparate disciplines, we have to follow a moving set of disciplines. I think a corporate model, or at least the old-fashioned corporate model, doesn't really capture what is good about and strong about discipline sets. Academics are very clever, and we will always do what is required to fit the current environment, but you end up measuring proxies of success rather than being successful. So we are good at maximizing proxies.

How do you build a great narrative/story for a novel idea? Is there a formula?

Storytelling and the power of narrative are really important. At CPC, we have a writer-in-residence scheme. We have some very distinguished, creative writers here. It strikes me how similar our processes are. As scientists, we are constrained by our evidence; however, as a creative writer, you are not. You can do whatever you want, but it is still about how to tell a compelling story. Telling a compelling story is important no matter who your audience is. Whether it's a specialist in your own discipline or whether it is a member of the general public, telling the story in the right way is equally significant. There is a public perception about science – people believe it is somehow objective and non-creative. Now this is absolutely not true. Inspired understanding of what the data is telling you is as creative as any other human endeavor. Young scientists often struggle with how to tell a story. They think that if you are true to the data, you have to tell the story in the order in which you did the experiments. But the best narrative may actually require starting off with the last experiment you did. The data has not changed in any way – only the order in which the story is told. The narrative pathway is often the last thing to emerge in the process of discovery. This is what happens with a writer. Writers write novels and they end up completely changing the structure and order of it because it works better if you do that – but they are not constrained by the data.

As a result, telling a scientific narrative is not the same as slavishly follow-ing the order in which you did perform the study. That seems obvious, but it is not. You can take the same set of data, give it to different storytellers, and end up with a paper that is able to be published in a much higher-ranking journal as a skilled teller has written it. This does not mean that you have oversold the data; you have just told it in a more compelling way or you have interpreted it in a more interesting way. The thing that gives me the biggest kick and I enjoy most as a scientist is being able to draw links that were not obvious, or to take a standard understanding and turn it on its head. I enjoy being able to say, "Well, actually, if you are going to use X to claim this, why don't you turn it on its head?" As a result, the interpretation is different to what everybody else thinks, and that is profoundly important. We've done this several times and it's always extremely uncomfortable. You are telling a whole field that the way they think about the world is not how the world is. This is hard, because intellectually vested interests usually become offended. On the other hand, this also makes it exciting intellectually and challenging as you are fighting against the prevailing way of thinking. We've done that in several fora over the years. It's even harder when you're considered the interloper. As an interloper, you have come into that discipline and pointed out something that is often obvious but has gone unap-preciated. Now you have disrupted their fields and this can be uncomfortable for both sides.

Does it concern you to enter all these new fields?

No, it is often compellingly clear that it is the right thing to do. Let me give you an example. Let's look at the obesity epidemic and its development since 1960, using the US as an example. Obesity has rapidly gone up since the 1960s; it really accelerated in the 1970s, 1980s, and 1990s. People often ask, why has it increased?

The first thing that most people agree on is that it is an energy imbalance, there are more calories in than calories out. Sure, it is partly because we expend fewer calories due to changes in lifestyle, and there is certainly something there. But, overwhelmingly, it is because we eat more calories than we ever used to. If you look at the breakdown of those calories, there are three principal sources: protein, carbohydrate, and fat. These three are the calorie-yielding macronutrients. If you look at the world's intake of those macronutrients, protein has remained remarkably stable across that time. The change in protein intake is nowhere near sufficient to account for the increase in calories that are being consumed. As a result, people have argued about whether obesity has principally been caused by fat or carbohydrates, both of which have gone up a lot. In some countries, one has gone up more than the other. Therefore, there has been this long-standing and really ferocious debate about whether it is fat or carbohydrate that caused obesity. Sugar or fat.

This debate has driven public policy and food manufacturing behaviors, and overall it has led to perverse outcomes. When were urged to eat less fat in the 1970s, we obliged. Food manufacturers replaced the fat with sugar, so obesity kept going up and up and up. In the mid-2000s, I worked alongside my long-standing collaborator, David Raubenheimer, who is now here at the CPC. Together we said, "Well, all our work on locusts, and mice, and all manner of other species shows that animals are able to regulate their intake of protein, fat, and carbohydrates separately." We drew the conclusion that they have appetites for these three things. If the protein intake has stayed the same, rather than saying it therefore can't be the cause of the obesity epidemic, we pointed out that actually, it could be the very reason why is it the cause of the obesity epidemic. If it has remained so stable, that indicates that it has been regulated in its intake. If you couple that observation (for which we have evidence from many other species that it is the case) with the fact that the principal shift in the human diet in that period had been to incorporate more and more processed foods, fat, and carbohydrate in the food supply, we realize that what we have done, essentially, is dilute protein. And you can measure by how much, and track that over time.

What that means is that if you have diluted protein in the diet, but our bodies maintain the intake as consistent, we have had to eat more calories to do that. Protein has leveraged calorie intake through our maintaining its intake consistent. Therefore, the fact that it is unchanged is the clue, not the reason for ignoring it. We call this the protein leverage hypothesis.[4] It quite literally turned the entire field on its head. In 2005, when the first paper was published, I was giving a talk at Cambridge. Afterward, one of the senior figures in human nutrition research came up to me. He said he had an admission; he had had to referee my manuscript. The manuscript had taken six months to come back to us with comments, and at the time we kept saying, "What's happening?" This senior figure told me he had blocked it and sat on it. He said he found it so outrageous that he was offended by it. Eventually, he did tell me we were right. He admitted we had noticed something that the rest of the field should have, but that we had to appreciate it was hard for them. I thought that was a very generous thing for him to say. It was an example of taking the same observations, coming up with an alternative way of looking at it, and changing an entire field.[5] And the people in that field find that hard.

Notes

1 An account of the principles of operation of the CPC is contained in Simpson, S. (2017). A systems approach to public health. *Journal and Proceedings of the Royal Society of New South Wales, 150*(463/464), 61–67.
2 Serendipity is indeed a source of innovation. You need to be prepared in order to interpret the stimuli from the environment, hence a breadth of previous experiences is crucial.
3 See also Cindy Tripp's interview on the need to have different metrics to reward individuals who are responsible for innovation within corporate settings.
4 The original research has been published in Simpson, S., & Raubenheimer, D. (2005). Obesity: the protein leverage hypothesis. *Obesity Reviews, 6*(2), 133–142.
5 This is another great example of how framing does indeed help in creative innovative hypotheses.

14
PAUL SLEZAK

Innovation is not a quick light switch. Sometimes innovation is about ensuring people are in a role where they can shine and giving them the opportunity to make suggestions and run with them.

Paul Slezak is the cofounder and CEO of RecruitLoop, an online recruitment platform giving employers a smarter way to hire. The platform provides a totally flexible and stress-free recruitment solution charged at an hourly rate. It also enables employers to automate and outsource the recruitment process on demand. Since launching in Sydney in 2011, RecruitLoop has saved clients millions compared to traditional recruitment. It has grown an engaged community of more than 6,500 expert recruiters across 60 countries, with more than 1,500 clients ranging from start-ups to Fortune 500 companies.

Before RecruitLoop, Paul was an Asia Pacific Regional Director at Aquent, an international recruitment firm headquartered in Boston, MA, USA.

Paul has experienced international success in the highly competitive recruitment industry by applying his professionalism, drive, and creativity to developing and delivering solutions that exceed business expectations. He also pushes the boundaries to create innovative solutions. He was able to forge a presence in these markets by demonstrating the ability to inspire key decision makers, executive management, clients, colleagues, and team members alike through his passion, enthusiasm, and commitment toward all those with whom he comes into contact.

What is innovation to you?

To me, innovation is very holistic, and it is not necessarily product innovation or purely technological innovation. Before you think about how to innovate your product or sales efforts, it is important that you have the right people doing the right things. If they are not, move them around as you would on a chessboard and then see what happens. You might find that they shine and create amazing products for you.

For example, we had an intern who we thought would be very suitable for a specific role. We thought she would perform brilliantly, but I realised she was getting very bored after three months. To inspire her interest again, I gave her another project to do which was completely outside of the original scope. This led to a huge impact on the business. The public would not have seen what she did, but the "innovation of people" was evident, as we didn't lose her. Instead, we got so much more out of her, and she developed and learned a lot. This is a case of innovating with not just technology but also your human capital.

I am always about "innovation of people." If you are speaking to someone who's an ENFJ or an ENTP in Myers–Briggs,[1] they are going to be completely different. One of them will not even think of the innovation of people and will be purely thinking of innovation, considering how we change things in the financial model or in the product model, but not with human capital.

We had a case where someone was working in one particular role, but he was not suited for that role. As a result, everyone was telling me to get rid of him. And I said, "No, create a new role for him where his strengths are." And four years later, he had excelled. To me, that was innovation. We created a role in an organization that played immensely to somebody's strengths and created an entirely new business strain that we would never have thought about. To me, that is innovation. We are seeing what someone's capabilities are, letting them run wild, and not firing them because they were not doing the right job that we originally gave to them. Instead, we are putting them in a new role and creating a new structure around them. This has resulted in their creating a new revenue stream which is now contributing to about a third of our business. Now *that* is innovation.

Where do you find sources of inspiration for new ideas or opportunities?

In my experience, I have found innovative ideas from the most random people in the company. For example, the customer success team, the research team in the Philippines, and an intern who came to us for six months may be the most innovative people in this very technology-driven company. When you allow somebody to get to know your business, you should ask them what they would think or they would do differently if given the opportunity. As they are looking at something with a completely blank canvas, they don't know the backstory, they don't know the original ideas. They just see what something is today and what it could become (in their mind) tomorrow.

One of them said to me, "I was looking at this specific page on our site. I think we should say this, and I think we should actually change the messaging to this, and try and do this." Now, this is somebody who has never really voiced her opinion. She is brilliant in what she does, but I thought, "Oh, my God. Where does that come from? That is absolutely genius."

It was someone who you would never bring to an innovation table, but someone who had some incredible ideas that are not only right but would actually not cost anything to implement. These changes could probably be designed and released in about a week. It is simple, and I said to her, "This is simple, but it is game-changing." After seven years of running the business, it took someone who had a classic employee mentality – she did not want to shine or say anything controversial – to come up with something amazing. We were having a one-to-one meeting and she said, "I just want to ask you something about this page. What does it mean?" It just spun off from there. She came up with ideas that were relatively simple to implement, but they were game-changing for the way they allowed us to connect with customers and develop an attraction for our platform.

Do you have any beliefs about innovation that might not necessarily be held by others?

People too often mistake innovation as a pivot. A pivot sometimes comes out of sheer desperation while clutching for your last breath. Innovation, on the other hand, is far more strategic, planned out, and worked through. Also, it is not a quick light switch – you cannot innovate just by doing. There must be a process behind it. Are you phasing something down and building something up? Are you doing it at the same time, and then you will shut that one off when this one's ready? I've seen so many of these start-ups go, "Oh, we're doing a pivot," and then they shut down. In circumstances where it is a pivot, I do not believe that it was an innovation piece. I would think that it was a fluke pivot. Although people will say, "Oh, we innovated …," in reality they did not innovate. This is where a "true" tech start-up CEO and I would go head-to-head, because they will say that is true innovation, and I would say it is not innovation. I would say that it was a desperate cry to try to make this product work. Therefore, it is not innovation, because they probably did it without consulting anybody.

The real innovation piece is, within your team of people, giving everybody the same right to speak up if they think something could be done better. It is not necessarily the product changing. It could be the change in workflow, it could be the change in messaging, or it could be the change in positioning; nothing in the product has to change at all. This is where I would completely disagree with people in the tech industry on what innovation actually is. Innovation does not have to be a rebuild or a completely new product. It does not have to be a new revenue stream. It can be tweaking something to make a very different impact by considering the people suggesting it and the ultimate user. We are not going to be building anything different there at all.

Innovation does not necessarily mean having to start again or do a complete reiteration. Innovation can be subtle and basic, as something basic can be game-changing.[2] Innovation is game-changing, but it does not have to be complex. It doesn't have to involve 18 engineers redesigning something. It doesn't have to involve a pivot; it can just be a small shift in the messaging, in the look and feel, in the workflow, or in the content layout of a page on a website.

Businesses need to be innovative but at the same time get things done today; that is, they have a portfolio of opportunities to invest in for both the short and the long term. How should a business balance the short-term necessities and the long-term goals? What has been your personal experience in approaching this particular challenge?

To me, this comes down to the human side of things. Each week, I sit down with an individual team member to look at short-term necessities and long-term goals. Many, many years ago I learned that in recruitment, you need to ask employees if there is anything they noticed or have done, in the last week, that could have been done differently. This can be within their job or within the wider company. They get quite shocked at first. They are thinking, what do you mean? You are asking me for my opinion on how the business should change? My answer is always yes.

Although I do not directly work on innovation, I look at innovating all the time because it means I am innovating myself as well. Also, I ask myself questions in a different way.[3] Usually, people would ask: how can I innovate my products? Then, then how can I innovate myself? And only after then, some would ask whether there are innovative ways to perform as a team. I do start with the team. Then I go, "Am I doing my best?" After you have innovated the way your team operates and yourself, it will all flow on down to the innovation of the business itself.

How do you create an environment/culture that cultivates creativity and innovation?

I like to give people the opportunity to speak up and make suggestions, and do that in whatever way they are comfortable. These suggestions are taken in the confidential forum around their own job, around what they are doing in the business, and also the direction of the business. Regardless of how valuable the suggestion is or is not, they need to know that you are thinking about it. You do not just say, "Thanks for the idea," and sweep it under the carpet. If you have to be honest and say, "We are not going to do anything with it," you have to say it and manage them accordingly. On the other hand, if they are suggesting something and it is really appropriate, I am not going to claim the changes. Instead, I will publicly recognize them for their contribution. Therefore, when the team notices the change and sees that an employee was recognized for it, they are inspired to contribute.

Can you think of examples where companies have innovated based on the needs of existing employees or customers?

Innovation is about people. It is about how they observe the world around them and create hypotheses of what can be done next as a company. Here are two examples.

Is going into food delivery an innovation for Uber? Absolutely. Why did they do that? They had drivers that did not have communication skills.[4] They wanted them to just drive around food and not communicate. In this case, the customers are a box of burgers.[5] Therefore, the passenger cannot give feedback. I think they just said, "How do we innovate our product? Why don't we deliver food, because it can't talk?" In my opinion, UberEats is easy. It is not very clean cars, drivers with little communication skills that can pick up a Chinese take away and drop it at someone's house.

That is what I thought as an observer of a new product launch. I think that UberEats is product innovation. I have realized that of every 100 lifts I get, there are 10 or 15 drivers that do not say a word to me and that have dirty cars. After the lift, I give all of that feedback. So maybe they thought, "Gosh, instead of switching these people off, a pizza box does not need a clean car. Give them a different purpose. Pay them a bit differently, but it does not matter if they hate speaking or if they have their heavy metal music on in the car and piss the customer off. It is not going to piss off a box of noodles."

Dropbox did the same thing. They started off with this repository where people could put their photographs and their documents. Dropbox wanted to beat email but initially could not. Now, following 18 months of innovation, they have launched Paper and they are going head-to-head with Google Docs. Head-to-head on complete file share. That was an innovation from the customers' use perspective.

There are a couple of food apps in America that initially started off sort of like UberEats but have now gone down a different path. After morphing through innovation, these companies are now offering the delivery of three meals a day. Fixed meals. If you want to get *anything* today, that is what you are getting today. It will never be the same day after day, and you can't order anything specific. There is a set option for breakfast, lunch, and dinner. That's it. It offers a healthy component via a level of nutritional value. That was true product innovation based on the customer. We do not offer everything, we offer one thing each day and that gets delivered.[6]

How do employees pitch ideas to you?

When somebody presents a new idea, they firstly say it to me. Then I get them to storyboard the idea, either via a drawing or a PowerPoint presentation. I want them to show why they're thinking that and whether it's screenshots or workflow. That way I know they haven't just had a fleeting idea but they've actually thought it through. That will be the impact that it has on their job and ultimately, the user. In our case, the user can be the recruiter or the customer. It's not just, "Oh, I've got this idea, how about this?" You need to be able to demonstrate the idea. For example, how more thought has gone into it, how will we use it, who will use it, and why will they use it? It can be as simple as three sheets, it can be three boxes, it can be four arrows, but they've thought it through. They realize that I am taking it seriously as I get them to actually put some thought behind it.

Are there any principles, techniques, processes, or other things that might be good in theory but haven't worked in practice in your experience?

Companies often wonder how they can make the innovation process more effective and what the innovation process is within the business. It dovetails off your employees. So we went in with one particular sales process in mind. When I realized the capacity, capability, and approach of the people, we innovated from there. If I made people do what I thought they should do, they would have all left. They would have hated what they do. I looked at their current skill sets. We became more of a sales-operational organization and kept our sales people. We were not doing the classic cookie-cutter sales approach. We didn't innovate the product, we innovated the way we were promoting it based on the people we had. Others would have said it was a complete waste of time and that we should have fired them. They would have told us to bring in new people and make them do as we asked. I don't do it like that. In my opinion, there is technology innovation and then there is process innovation.

There is also human capital innovation, which is about innovating the strength, competencies, and the behaviors of your people.[7] The people most passionate about the product are the ones who built it, the CTOs or heads of product. That is design thinking. That is product innovation. That is very different to changing a strategy, the work flow, or the operational processes, which always reflect who's doing them rather than changing the people.

When you are investigating your different pillars, you should be really aiming for true product people to talk about the product innovation. Then maybe talk to COOs around operational innovation. Finally, you will have people like me. We wear the human capital innovation hat. You will get very different ideas, but I think that is what makes it worthwhile.

Notes

1 The Myers–Briggs test is a well-known personality profile test, also known as the MBIT test. It classifies personality across fours dimensions: introversion and extroversion; intuition and sensing; feeling and thinking; and perceiving or judging. Some research has been done on the relation between personality type and innovation, but there is no substantial evidence. See Killen, D., & Williams, G. (2009). *Introduction to Type and Innovation*: CPP.

2 Innovation does not necessarily need to be measured in terms of how novel it is in comparison to current practices. In this case, Paul refers to an important aspect of innovation, which is the focus on the outcome of the new practices, products, and services. Sometimes, something that is overlooked and taken as given can be modified and provide sizable outcomes. For a similar (yet different) concept, refer to Frugal Innovation and the process of achieving more with fewer resources, or eliminating non-essential features in a product to sell to developing countries.

3 Paul is using a well-known technique here, re-framing the question, from an individual to a team perspective.

4 While we don't know whether UberEats was born out of this observation, this is a great example of reframing in order to generate new opportunities. What if the

customer is a box? What if the customer is an inanimate object? These questions will help you think about different kinds of customers for your business.

5 Imagine that you were Uber and were doing an innovation activity. What if the customer is an object rather than a human being? What you are doing here is again reframing the problem from a different perspective. For other framing techniques, see Garbuio, M., Dong, A., Lin, N., Tschang, T., & Lovallo, D. (2018). Demystifying the genius of entrepreneurship: How design cognition can help create the next generation of entrepreneurs. *Academy of Management Learning & Education, 17*(1), 41–61.

6 As in the case of disruptive innovation, innovation is often providing less, offering lower performance or fixed choices rather than offering more than competitors. Over time, as long as you are on a path of fast learning, you can better understand your customers and offer always something more exciting, while also solving any supply chain problems you might have. In this regard, the history of Netflix is remarkable.

7 If you are interested in personalities and innovation, see Schilling, M. A. (2018). *Quirky: The Remarkable Story of the Traits, Foibles, and Genius of Breakthrough Innovators Who Changed the World*: PublicAffairs. A tip from us: If you are thinking about organizing a workshop or a brainstorming session, it is a good idea to invite everyone to think about defining the problem (not generating solutions!) before the session or, at the very start of the session, to write down ideas individually rather than as a group. Then, you can ask them to work in pairs before working as a group. In this way you can capture the power of introverts in idea generation.

15

ANDRÉ TEIXEIRA

I like to work in the intersections. Crossroads are the best vantage point to reflect about intriguing ideas and potential innovations.

Dr Teixeira is an Associate Partner with Globalpraxis in Barcelona, Spain, and an Executive Professor of Innovation at the Antwerp Management School of the University of Antwerp in Belgium and CEIBS in Switzerland. Additionally, he is a partner at Keiryo Packaging, a start-up in Luxembourg, and Wine With Spirit, an award-winning innovative wine start-up in Portugal.

Previously, Dr Teixeira was General Manager, Innovation at Bundaberg Brewed Drinks in Australia; Chief R&D and Quality Officer with Goodman Fielder Ltd, Australia; Entrepreneur in Residence with CSIRO, Australia; President of Coca-Cola Russia, Ukraine, and Belarus in Moscow, Russia; Managing Director of Coca-Cola Services (Europe) in Brussels; Vice President, Global Innovation and Development at Interbrew (subsequently InBev); and Vice President Research & Development (International) at the Campbell Soup Co. He also worked for Coca-Cola for 23 years in 5 continents, in positions ranging from R&D, Innovation, and Operations to General Management. A creator of an ideation technique now used worldwide and of a management development program based on the Classics, Dr Teixeira publishes regularly in the specialized press, and he is a frequent guest speaker at conferences worldwide.

What is innovation to you?

I always prefer not to talk about innovative ideas, but rather focus on the concept of *intriguing ideas*. They are the frequent and recurrent raw material for the innovative concepts and projects that one can derive from them. If we focus on intriguing ideas, we have a head start on what might eventually become an innovative avenue of thought for a great new concept.

One example that comes to mind is the work we were involved in a few years ago in creating the basis of a new product offering for a major airline. An interesting insight was that the airline in question had a higher than usual proportion of women flying their business class in long-haul flights. The intriguing idea was how they could differentiate their product from the competition by creating mechanisms to attract and retain even more business women. A series of add-ons were created, which without exception focused on women and tested well with women, and the overall experience of their business class was enhanced, without alienating the still prevailing majority of male business travelers.

To me, a business class product in an airline is not just about getting you from point A to point B. This is what DHL does. DHL and FedEx will ship a box from Amsterdam to Shanghai. And it will be delivered, and it is fine. But the business class on an airline is about making you feel refreshed and ready for business, with your mind clear and looking good. And that is why we tried to change the way the business class looked at most business people. They are not interested in incredibly good food or fantastic wines. I mean, I do not go to a restaurant to fly, so I do not go to an airline to eat. But if you have a comfortable seat, if you have services that make you feel refreshed with a clear mind when you get there, that is what it is all about. And that is what we are trying to do with this product. This is an ongoing project. After that, they expanded this to other aspects, in which I was only indirectly involved. They did a club for destinations. So, if you are flying to, say, China, all the people that normally fly to China, they would have that commonality of interests. With exchange, they would have business opportunities coming out of that. They would have cultural insights into doing business there. So, the airline became not just a mean of transportation, but the key to understanding your destination and connecting people.

What is the one thing that you do regularly (e.g., daily, quarterly, annually) which has contributed to your success in spotting innovative ideas/ solutions?

I like to work at the intersections. Crossroads are the best vantage point to reflect about intriguing ideas and potential innovations. If I can force myself, as I do regularly, to appreciate or even create an intersection of science and technology with cognitive, sensorial, psychological, and other aspects of the overall human experience, then I am on to something new or at least something very interesting to think about.

What I force myself to do every day, in any aspect of life, even if I am looking at this coffee here, I think about the extraction, the technology, what could make it more special. And I combine this technology, or the scientific thinking about the product itself, with an experiential element to that, a psychological aspect, or an insight that you have, or a sensorial experience. If you can mix those things, that is normally where you find the best opportunities.[1]

That is the same for our age of enlightenment in which we live. Let's face it, if we were born 200 years ago, we would be believing in witches in the forests. We would be believing that earthquakes were caused because you had pagans in the city. So, if we focus on reason, and we focus on science, which are irrefutable facts and, at the same time, we focus on humanism to know that we are here for a reason, that is exactly the kind of progress we need to move us forward. This balance of facts and science with a humanistic view is what will keep us in the direction of good innovation.

Sometimes the best innovation is in front of you. It is a question of observing but knowing how to separate facts from the impact that those facts have. Everybody has the right to have their opinions, but not everybody has the right to have their own facts. Facts are facts. I do not have a problem with opinions. You can give me any opinion in the world. But facts are facts. That cannot be changed. The risk we have today is that these alternative facts, which have been created, are clouding our ability to see innovation opportunities because people believe that innovation is just a map, when it is not.

That is why I like the concept of intersection as a practice. "What do I know about economics and what do I know about psychology? And where can I find some economics and psychology that I can intersect? If I am an engineer, what do I know about some engineering or physics or science and how that intersects with the human experience?" At the intersections is where you find some of the best innovation opportunities. Not just in products, but also services and business models.

Where do you find sources of inspiration for new ideas or opportunities?

I like to find sources of inspiration in going completely outside of the specific category I am working with. If you look at most businesses, most people are working on innovations. So if you work in cosmetics, what do they do? They go to a shop to look at cosmetics. If they work in beverages, they go to a supermarket. They look at the beverage aisle. I never like to do that. What I like to do is to go completely outside of my zone of comfort and look for opportunities there. We were asked to develop a line of beverages that were seasonal, that would be changing every three months according to the season. There was a beverage for winter, summer, spring, and autumn. And my inspiration was to take my team to Milan and Paris for fashion shows with the aim to highlight creative thinking. Why's that? Because, as opposed to most industries, the fashion industry, by definition, if it is very successful this season, it will have to change everything for the next season. You cannot say "Here is what I launched for this winter. Guess what? I am going to repeat that next year." No! Which is different from almost any other product, which you want to keep as long as you can. So, by understanding the keys and the cues that they have in terms of color, in terms of insights, in terms of materials, and how that can be construed into something completely different, that is how we came up with the seasonal products.

They are almost like self-destructing products. They would self-destroy if they were a success.

What unlikely sources of inspiration have you discovered that surprisingly helped you solve an important problem or be creative?

I was working for a well-known multinational and we had to launch a line of new beverage products. Frozen carbonated slushies were a major investment by a significant customer. We needed to create something that would be not just a new line of products but rather a new experience for the consumers, mainly youngsters, buying a refreshment after school in a major urban area in Asia. In observing them when they purchased the products, I became aware that almost without exception they smelled the product before slurping them. At the same time, we were launching the product line, a chain of movie theaters in Hong Kong was experimenting with a sensorial novelty: the introduction of smells and fragrances in the air-conditioning ducts of their cinemas. So if there were battle scenes, a smell of gunpowder would come through. If you had a scene in a green field, you'd have the smell of the green field. So we decided to do the same. Every time we changed over to a new flavor in the convenience stores where we were selling the products, we introduced exactly the same fragrance in the air-conditioning pipes. So if it were raspberry, the whole store would delicately smell like fresh raspberries. When the kids came into the store, they would smell the raspberry, and they would then go straight to that machine, almost as if they were led by the Pied Piper of Hamelin. It was unbelievable. The next month the stores would be smelling like orange, or mango, or whatever. It was very interesting. But again, it was an unlikely source of inspiration, because it was the theater. But at the end of the day, it was the same thing, because actually, what we created was the theater of experience. Drinking that product or slurping that product was kind of a theatrical thing. The smell only helped that.

It goes back to the idea of intersections and psychology, and the idea of looking outside of your area of comfort. Look for inspiration completely opposite, not where you're comfortable with. And the other thing that normally happens in my view with innovation that is quite different, and anybody who wants to work with us should know, is that there is a significant amount of violation of rules when you innovate. You cannot innovate by just following rules. You have to break rules. When canned coffee was launched in Japan in the late 1970s, we were violating a number of rules by which coffee is judged, because you judge coffee on the ritual, on the aroma, on the smell, on the whole experience of that. And all of a sudden, we trapped this whole thing in a can which is not very sexy, not very ritualistic, but we created other rituals. For instance, we launched it in hot and cold vending machines, so that in the winter people would buy two hot cans and use them as hand-warmers in the train stations before drinking them. So, we created a new ritual. You have to go out and break rules. When you break rules, then things start showing some progression.

Who do you generally approach to get a fresh perspective on an idea or otherwise to validate an idea?

Consumers are not very good at telling us what they will want. They are good at telling us what they want. So I like to approach consumers as co-creators and not necessarily as filters. You have people always saying, "Ask the consumers, the consumers will tell you." The consumers won't tell you. Consumers will tell you what they want now. They won't tell you what they will want. Never ever. So, you have to use them as co-creators at a particular stage of the process. In my methodology, I start with the internal people enriching ideas. Then I go to a level of expertise that tends to narrow. Expertise in innovation of consumer goods doesn't help in expanding; expertise narrows. Expertise is good if you're going to have a brain operation. You don't want somebody who's curious about it. You want an expert, right? I mean, in science it is the same. If you are developing a new theory of quantum mechanics, you need a person who's an expert. But in consumer goods and innovation for products and services, you normally need to have people that are non-experts, to begin with, then you bring the experts to put it on a track. And then you use consumers as co-creators in the process.

When you or your team have identified new ideas, how do you select the ones to pursue and the ones to discard? Is there a set approach or methodology?

I like to operate with my own methodology that involves specific criteria of enrichment through a series of concentric circles, followed by the application of criteria on three fronts: differentiation, relevance, and resonance.

After enriching the ideas, we look for levels of differentiation and levels of relevance, and now I am using the third criterion, which is resonance. How do we expect that idea to resonate with potential users? If we then measure that, even subjectively – we have to be careful in these things, because it is almost like someone asks, "Do you love me 33% more this year than you did last year?" If the person says yes and you believe in it, then you both know you're lying and he's lying. But we're both happy, right? But we have to understand that it is a subject of measurement. And the fact that you put an objective measurement in front of a subjective judgment doesn't make the subjective judgment objective. It is still subjective, but it is a starting point. So it is a way of measuring. As the philosophers say, "If triangles had a god, that god would be in the shape of a triangle." Right? It is the same thing here. So we have numbers to measure things, and that is how we do it. What we try to do is to measure how different it is, how relevant it is.

Relevance is something that is meaningful to an existing or a potential application. Is this utilitarian? Is this something that people can make use of it? Is it something that solves a problem? Is this something that addresses a vacuum? That sort of thing. So, if it is relevant, then you can measure that on a scale. But again, it is very subjective. It is just a starting point. And what you do with that is establish some criteria. And it is funny to see how people react to what is relevant. We do this online using Zeetings. Zeetings is this website that I use in classrooms a lot. Zeetings.com enables people to vote with their cellphones online. And that also solves the problem of those people who cannot be without their cellphones for two hours. They start trembling if it is not in their hands. So we make them use the cellphone by voting for some of these ideas that they have collectively enriched, for relevance, for differentiation. And resonance is how is it expected to resonate with a particular group of people.

This is particularly true when you do technological things. Some technology is not visible. You do not think about the fact that this glass bottle that I am holding here, probably had a weight that was three times the weight it has now about 100 years ago. It still contains the same water. It is still the same shape. But it has three times less glass in it than it did 100 years ago. If you say that, people say, "Yeah, yeah, it is relevant." It doesn't resonate because people don't remember how heavy it was 100 years ago, because you were not there. Nobody knows. So that is a classic case. You need to try to measure how – and also to know that when things resonate with a group of people, it resonates for a certain period of time. And then it becomes part of the expected, taken for granted. Remember when cars used to have an ABS badge? Now, not a single car has ABS written on it, because you take it for granted that all cars will have ABS (antilock braking system). And power steering? I remember my father's car had power steering written on the side of the car. And I don't think I have driven a car without power steering for a long, long time.

What is the most important thing(s) that organizations need to change in order to be more open to new ideas or approaches?

I think that the best thing organizations can do about innovations is to accept the statistics. Ninety-nine percent of what happens in innovation is failure. And to think that everything you're going to do is going to be successful is ridiculous. Begin by measuring return on investment and net present value, for example. Net present value is a measure that assumes that the product is going to be there forever, which is ludicrous because in some consumer goods it lasts three months. Those measures are critical, but it is all a question of when to apply them. They need a virtual P&L for innovation, and they need to accept that the rule in innovation is failure; success is the exception, not the other way around. Trying to calculate ROIs on innovation when you hardly have finished elaborating on an idea is an exercise in futility.

So I created a virtual P&L. In some businesses in the past, what I did was I created the concept of a company within a company. So we all became shareholders of the company, the whole innovation team. And we have a P&L, which we agreed with the business, that for every product we launched successfully I would take a percent of that, which would be a small royalty, a fake royalty like a Bitcoin royalty, and we would bring that into our revenue line. And our costs were our expenses line. And then we tried to, at least, break even, and then we started having people realizing the success of the product concerns them because part of the calculation of their bonuses I made on the result of that virtual P&L. So they became really as if they were shareholders. It was like a company across the street.

I remember the CEO of the business came to me, because they became interested in this concept. And he said, "Yeah, it'is all very nice, but I cannot go to another company across the street and get those services. I can only come to you." And I said, "Yes, that is true, but on the other hand, I can't go to our main competitor and sell it to them. I can only sell it to you." So it is like being married with kids. You have your crises, but you put up with them. That is how it is. So in the end it worked very nicely. We started the biggest cultural shift, from an innovation psychology point of view, where you start putting effort behind where there was more value. Most people, particularly scientists and technologists, tend to put more effort behind where there is more difficulty. Because of the challenge of the difficulty, they put more effort there, whereas, in innovation, you need to put more effort behind where there is more value. Sometimes the most value comes from very easy things, not from the most difficult things, so it is quite an interesting change in psychology.

Part of the problem is in the difference between budgeting for today. How can you do all this when you have to do all the things you need to do today? You have to justify your existence. Innovative people are expensive. How can you justify having all these people dealing with the future? And nobody has an experience with the future, right? So, everybody is like Indiana Jones, "Trust me, we're going to be successful in that." And then, how can you do all of that if you have to deliver results today? And I think that is where the difference, again, is a financial option. You say, "You budget for today, but invest for the future." An investment has risks, but you have to separate budget from investment. And you have to always find in what you do that low-hanging fruit.

From your experience, do you think that the same people that work for the current need and the non-disruptive part should be, or could be, the same people that work for the most disruptive work?

It's a scale. You have those who definitely should be only in the day-to-day things. People working with efficiencies, working with all that sort of thing. Then you have those who really break through barriers, eliminators, people who are disruptive types. And you have the middle, the hybrids. My recommendation is always to say, "Keep the hybrids to a manageable size, because hybrids are always risky." These hybrids, many of them, don't want to be in innovation for a long time. They want to go into marketing. They want to go somewhere else. They want to do day-to-day things. They are driven by certain types of motivations. They are, from a psychological point of view, they're schizoids, which is fine. If you're a schizophrenic and happy, it is not a problem in innovation. Because they are people who can juggle the business needs with the barrier disruption.

On the other hand, if you only have hybrids in your group, you're never going to have a disruption, and you're not going to solve any problems. So I would say that keeping those hybrids is important. Remembering that hybrids are always very risky. I've been a hybrid my whole life, and I know how risky that is. Because you have the risk of the day-to-day people thinking that you are a dreamer, and the real scientists and people like that, they think you're "just" a business person. So you're neither here nor there. But it is critical to keep a balance and, most importantly, you have to hire different groups. You cannot hire someone who can do everything. So you have to know what you're hiring. To me, that is the essence of where you can make the most mistakes in organizations – hiring for the same thing. They hire for an R&D position. They hire for an innovation position. Or they say, "No, no. R&D will report to marketing," which is very, very dangerous. Or vice versa, of course. Particularly, nowadays, with the change in the sets of skills that you need, you need new skills. With artificial intelligence taking a lot of the routine jobs out of the way, we need to retool ourselves. And we need to be looking for completely new skills that will create that kind of new profession. And the hybrids are going to excel. Because no computer will replace the hybrids. Computers will replace a lot of the routine work, analytical work, things like this. Computers will even replace some of the very creative things. When it comes to mathematical calculation, algorithms, chemical pathways, and all that. But they won't replace the hybrids. The hybrids will be able to switch between the two. So if I had to recommend to any youngster today to do anything in terms of an academic career, I would say do extremes. Go for extremes. Study biochemistry and psychology. Study economics and physics, and something like that. Law and medicine, or whatever. Because those hybrids are going to be the future.

Businesses need to be innovative but at the same time get things done today; that is, they have a *portfolio* of opportunities to invest in for both the short and the long term. How should a business balance the short-term necessities and the long-term goals? What have been your personal experiences in approaching this particular challenge?

The key differentiator is budget versus investment. You budget for today and you invest in the future. My personal experience has been that every time you have budgets being projected for a hopefully successful innovation, failure comes even faster. We all know hope is not a strategy. It is important to have an allocation for the future, a virtual P&L to elicit the sense of accountability of the innovation team and to make sure that the resources of the team are always allocated partially to solving some of the daily problems and identifying the low-hanging fruit.

How do you create an environment/culture that enables creativity and innovation?

Hire for innovation, manage failure well, do not isolate the team from daily chores, avoid the rush for immediate results, and create a sense of accountability by thinking of the innovation group as a company across the street rendering services to the main organization.

Innovation culture is always a difficult question. Because culture as always, from an anthropological point of view, is both a cause and a consequence, right? You have certain types of behavior, and certain types of attitudes, and certain types of patterns of action, and you do have a series of phenomenon that, put together, define a culture. So it is both a cause and a consequence. Do you create a culture for innovation? I don't think you can. I think what you can do is create an environment where that culture can gradually flourish. And one of the best things to do is to create, in my view, the idea that it is a company within a company – that is great accountability. Because the last thing you'll need is to have within a big company, for instance, to have a culture of people who are working in innovation, but they are all these civil servants that are there just doing the work, nine to five, "Yeah. Today, I have to think, so I will think." You need people who have this start-up mentality within even the biggest company.

Think about the last time you pitched (or have been pitched) an innovative idea or solution. What worked well and what didn't?

One of the most difficult things for the innovator is that when you're pitching something, you are pitching a belief, or a hope, or a potential. Beliefs, or hopes, or potentials are not strategies, right? When you're done pitching something that you hope is going to be okay, or that you believe is going to be okay, you have to find a way of capturing people's imaginations, and not just their ability to calculate the logic. Hence, if you are a good innovator, you have to be ahead of your time. You cannot expect the audience, or the manager, or whoever is in charge to actually be ahead of his or her time, because that is not what he or she is paid for. They're paid to be here and now, to make the company profitable now. As they reminded me, time and time again, they paid my salary by being focused on the now. And my salary could not just be in the future, right? So an example of this is what worked and what didn't work. I'll do an example that didn't work. About 30 years ago, I had this idea that one of our products in our lineup in the company was present globally, but because of different taste preferences, and different food laws, and things like this, the product tasted different everywhere.

The product was a beverage. In Belgium, for instance, it contained 10% juice, had no color, was very light. In Germany it was 15% juice and red in color. In Spain, it was almost fully red. In the US, it was very artificial in appearance. And then people would travel and would say, "Oh, I tasted this product in that country, and that country. It tastes quite different. When can we have that here? It was very nice." I had the idea of doing a world thing, that we would do this brand but from all over the world. I was in Hong Kong at the time as I was responsible for doing this innovation for Asia. And then I said, "Why don't we launch for three months the Orange from Jamaica, then for three months Orange from Brazil, or from Mexico, or from France, and keep rotating these things, and keeping a lot of interest in the product?" And the idea was to develop the products to be very much similar to meet the food laws, but the tastes would be different. But then it was killed. It was killed because I had visualized a world that was much ahead of my time.

In other words, at that time people traveling to Jamaica from somewhere in Asia would be a no-no. Traveling to Mexico was a unique thing. You do that if you are in the US. But Europeans or Asians were unlikely to go to Mexico. So we were much ahead of our time, and I did not take that into consideration. The idea was killed. Twenty years later they did exactly that and I was fascinated to see the way they did this. They still do that. They do all these flavors of the world and things like this because it is the stuff of dreams, in a way. People come back from their vacation, and they want to extend their vacation by keeping that taste with them. So they go to Spain and they taste Valencia orange products in Spain. They come back to Germany in the middle of the winter, and they drink that Valencia orange; they remember the Spanish sun.

How do you build a great narrative/story for a novel idea? Is there a formula?

I think there are two things to focus on here. First of all, we need to accept that storytelling is very important. You cannot just pitch an innovative idea only with the technicalities, the intrinsic details. Sometimes you have to leave that aside in order to be able to sell it. So, storytelling is very important.

However, the formula that exists is more a formula of how not to do it, than a formula of how to do it. It is like the news, right? If you say, "What is the right format for the news?" Is it CNN where you get these snippets of breaking news that you have to have repeated a few times before you understand what is going on and you have a ticker tape going underneath that forces you to listen to one news, read another one, and sometimes not know about any of those? Or, is this more like a BBC radio news that explains and gets to the point, goes slowly, and then stops, and gets to the next one? There's no magic answer here, but what you do know is that the North Korean news, that is the one you don't do, right? That is the one that doesn't mean anything. When presenting a new idea, a lot of people tend to do the North Korean news. In other words, this is the truth and I'll present you nothing but the truth, forgetting that what people are perceiving may be completely different.

Here are some formulas that you can eliminate. The most important one is that you never pitch an idea to a multidisciplinary audience and hope that everybody is going to capture everything. So do pre-pitching. What I have always done is that if I had what I considered to be potentially a big idea about some-thing and I wanted to present it, I would go to the marketing team and talk to them about the marketing story. I go to the engineers and I talk to them about the technical side of it. I go to the finance guys and say, "This may make sense," and ask, "How can you can help me formulate the virtual P&L here?" And then when you go to the general audience, they have all been briefed and they all hear what you already told them. Because if you go to a multidisciplinary audience and you start presenting this great thing you encounter the "yes-butters," those people who say, "Yes, but. Yes, but you cannot do this. Yes, but it is too expen-sive." So look for the "no-butters," the people that say no, "No, it is a stupid idea. But if you do this and that, it is going to work." No-butters are better people to have in a meeting than yes-butters when you are pitching something. When you do the big pitch to the multidisciplinary audience, it is almost the same as looking for investors. Investors do not need to understand the whole thing, they just need to buy into your story and they need to understand your vision.

Note

1 The importance of the sensorial experience is explicit in the work of Alessi, one of the Italian Factories of Design. This can be tested with almost "quantitative" evalu-ation tools. Alberto Alessi, the President of the company, states, "We have a very helpful tool that we call, ironically, "the formula." It's a mathematical model that we use once we have a well-done prototype. Not the first or the second prototype, but from the third one on. The purpose of the formula is to understand what the reaction of our final customers could be toward this new product and what the prod-uct's life could be should we decide to start production." See Alessi, A. (2016). *The Dream Factory: Alessi Since 1921.* Milan: Rizzoli. Capozzi, M., & Simpson, J. (2009). Cultivating innovation: An interview with the CEO of a leading Italian design firm. *The McKinsey Quarterly,* February 2009.

16
CINDY TRIPP

I think of innovation as something that has three components: new, meaningful, and useful.

Cindy Tripp serves as the President for her own company, Cindy Tripp & Company, which was founded in 2012. Cindy helps her clients to grow through innovation. The company offers a multitude of services, including leadership mentoring, design thinking workshops, and speaking and educational programs. One of Cindy's main priorities is to respect every individual, beyond just their work position. She believes that this respect can lead to increased creativity among individuals, which creates growth for the company as a whole. Tripp is an expert in design thinking and also serves as a strategist for two other companies, Lenora Polonsky and Associates and C-Suite Consulting-Partners Group. Prior to these positions, Cindy worked at Procter & Gamble for 24 years where she started the company's journey in design thinking. At P&G, she created a global network of individuals to assist with the implementation of design thinking techniques, eventually making P&G a frontrunner in the area of design thinking under the CEO at the time, A.G. Lafley. Cindy was one of the first people to connect the idea of design thinking to business strategy.

What is innovation to you?

I think of innovation as something that has three components: new, meaningful, and useful. It is a common misnomer that people say, "Oh, if it is an invention or if it is new, novel, it is an innovation." That is an incomplete definition. Being new, meaningful, and useful creates the healthy tension that design thinking holds itself accountable to, which is being human-centered instead of being new for new's sake. You can be new and inventive and creative that way, but I am not an inventor. I do not invent things, but I am really good at recognizing when something is meaningful and useful and cultivating the new.

In my view, businesses struggle at offering something new, meaningful, and useful at the same time. Often, they are struggling because they just want to get something new out there. I am talking to them about the meaningful and useful, and they are saying "Let's just do anything."

That is business pressure. The business pressure is we have to do something. Design thinking says activity for activity's sake is not going to lead to something that is really going to make a difference in the long term. You have to study the human in the system and discover the meaningful and useful.

So to me, that is what innovation is. It has all three components, and that is why I love it. Some people say, "Oh, it is those crazy wild ideas." But it is not just about crazy wild ideas. It is crazy wild ideas that are meaningful to someone and useful to them, and so I love those three things.

Going back to my P&G days, when I think about something new, meaningful, and useful, I think about the Swiffer idea, the whole Swiffer franchise of reimagining cleaning as something that can be joyful and fun. The team who worked on the Swiffer idea made little changes in invention and creativity in terms of the implements, but not dramatic change. The real innovation part of that equation was understanding the human in the equation, and what they needed, and what they wanted. I look at the Swiffer franchise and see how they have transformed cleaning into something that is no big deal. It is no big deal to take care of your home. They have made it a little fun, a little joyful. That would be an example of new, meaningful, and useful. First, they didn't change up the playing field. They reorganized, if you will, how you clean. The Swiffer WetJet changed even more – you did not need a bucket, and yet it didn't remain dirty after use. So there was some creativity in that. But to me, the thing that really pushed the envelope was the meaningful and useful, and that came from looking at humans in the system and how to make it better.

I found another example recently when I was working with a hospital client who had a system for how they discharged patients. What they saw in the system was resistance to going home. Healthcare says, "Time to go home," and the patient feels, "I'm not ready to go home." After some research, they thought they had an issue with information at the time of discharge. When I was brought into the project, instead of assuming that was the case, I suggested that we should study the whole system, and we started by looking at human needs. We discovered that it wasn't the information at discharge that was the issue. It was an issue that started from the moment they arrived at the hospital, when they were admitted. The issue was actually how the hospital navigated the entire care journey. In order to address the issue, they created a different algorithm, a different protocol. They created a new protocol for how they navigated through that, and reorganized some things, added some others. And as a result, their readmissions went down, and their patients' willingness to go home went up.

This is an example, again, of innovation. When I think about innovation, I get as excited about the innovation that is driven out of the meaningful and useful as I do about a cool new gadget. Obviously, when the iPhone came out, it was innovative in that it was incredibly new and different, but it was also meaningful and useful. People needed freedom to navigate because they were traveling more. It makes total sense to be able to have that power in your hands, and that required incredible invention.

I think people overlook the things like what I just talked about with Swiffer and with the hospital group I worked with. They overlook the power of just getting clearer with the human in the system. And so to me, innovation is both the Apple iPhone when it came out a decade ago, as well as a new hospital system that reduces readmissions, and a cleaning product that transforms a chore into something that is kind of fun. All of those to me are equal.

When you discover the meaningful and useful, you can give scientists the lighthouse of what needs to be created. When I first started at P&G in 1988, scientists were in their labs inventing, and they would throw it over the wall to marketing and say, "Market this." And I was the recipient of lots of those things that had no reason for being. Just because you can change the molecule does not mean you should. What's in it for the consumer? I saw a shift when marketing and research and design thinkers were studying the meaningful and useful, and setting what we call "desired consumer experiences"[1] and "standards of excellence".[2] I really prefer this model.

In my career at P&G, it flipped from scientists inventing stuff to people articulating desired consumer experiences and the standards of excellence of those experiences. In the mid-1990s, as that transition was happening, and about the same time that A.G. Lafley became CEO,[3] the company was beginning to realize that the consumer is the boss, that the human is the center. I worked on the first ever multifunctional R&D-led team looking into desired consumer experiences. I worked in baby care. At the time, diapers were all about containment. It was about how much fluid can they absorb in how little time. For this work, all over the world, we went into people's homes, spoke to mums and observed babies. This was a very different angle than looking at the diaper itself. When you change your focal point from the diaper to the baby and the mum in their environment, you see a lot differently. So we spent time creating the desired consumer experiences and setting those standards of excellence.

At the time we did this, Pampers was a plastic diaper and it had very little other functionality other than containment. So we looked at the way the diaper was being used at home, and we were curious, "Why is everything in the room soft and quiet except the diaper?" Because diapers woke kids up when they were plastic. You would open them and it would startle the baby awake. They came in a plastic bag, which had warnings on the label of "Do not have near children. May suffocate." All the human factors of the diaper experience said, "Do not touch me. Do not have me around your kids." That is when we started creating a new desired consumer experience and the standards of excellence in the world of baby care. We did that and then we built the segmentation of the types of mums within that. The work we did in 1996–1997 propelled the Pampers business and all of the innovation pipeline for the next decade, or beyond actually, and grew the business from about $2.7 billion to $10 billion in seven years. That is the kind of innovation that gets me excited because then the scientists had something to go chase. Let's go chase blanket softness. Let's go chase baby quiet. These became the new standards that drove everything. The thing about a desired consumer experience and a standard of excellence is that you may never actually reach it. They are meant to be aspirational. But if you move in that direction, you're increasing your ability to be meaningful and useful to the human that you're serving. So the invention is chasing the human.

Scientists continue to invent things against that model. But I did not get as excited about the inventions that people came up with, such as new material inventions. I get excited when people invent something which is meaningful and useful. So when I think about innovation, I feel like solving a math or chemistry problem is straightforward. I think scientists are well equipped to do that, and I have great confidence that they can if they know what they're look-ing for. I think that design thinking gives you a lot of that data, and what I now love doing is helping clients understand the meaningful and useful so that it does propel them over time versus when they just focus on invention. I could do a design thinking workshop for them and we could come up with a good one-off idea. That would be such a disservice to them to not do the fundamental work to see the picture of where we are headed. And then what can we do first? How can we build a sequence of events that puts us there? That is my innovation philosophy.

Of course there is the other side: we need people who are just out there tinkering and exploring. There is more than one way of creating advancement. Some companies default to the tinkering in inventing molecules versus a balance between tinkering and starting from the human, and I like to participate in the balanced approach. There are people who are investigating something like "Is there dark matter in the world"? I do not know. I would never know. But I love that they are asking that wild question and trying to figure it out and making dis-coveries. But my place in the world of innovation is thinking about the human.

Who do you generally approach to get a fresh perspective on an idea or otherwise to validate an idea?

To validate an idea is really a dilemma, especially in the world of business or organizations that are having to make these calls on what to invest in. When Febreze came out with the trigger nozzle for their Air Effects, the ability to encapsulate odor was an incredible invention. There was science behind Febreze, how it clears the air and how you could also spray it on things and it would change their smell. There was hard science in there, but there was a decision to change the form factor of the product to make it distinctive and more pleasurable for the user. And that form factor costs a lot of money for what BASES, who typically validated P&G's ideas, said would not grow any volume.[4]

The validation technique we had at P&G was BASES. And BASES said, "You are not going to get anything from that investment. It will not change your volume at all because we tested with and without it and there is no difference." The president of the business decided to do it on gut. Of course, he is the president of the business, he can make a gut decision. He had been in consumers' homes. He had talked to them about the human side of things. It was not arbitrary. In the market, this product was wildly successful. People loved using it because of the trigger action, and it was new and different. It was a wildly successful launch, and it really led them to their air-care strategy because Febreze had only been a fabric refresher before. And now they have a huge portfolio of products around air care, which is a much broader strategy than just fabric. All of that came from the president being willing to lean into what he knew was very valid for consumers, but he couldn't demonstrate it in his economics or in his validation techniques. Roger Martin has talked a lot about reliability versus validity, and I have found him inspiring on this.[5] Business is a reliability world, but innovation is a validity world.

The business world does not understand what validity is. They understand reliability because that is how they run their business, reliably predictable results. You can get a fresh perspective and validity for your idea by taking your ideas to the people who are intended to benefit from the idea and play catch ball with them. You can get their feedback, or better yet, have them help you develop ideas.

A process of co-creation occurs when we study one group, and we get insights, and we get ideas about what they're trying to achieve, and we create something. You may not go back to the people you studied originally, but you go to people with the goal of co-creation, and of course, that is magic all on its own.[6] You have to not be too formal. You have to engage them on a level playing field, you co-create, and that co-creation creates another opportunity to validate that you are on the right path, that you are doing something that is meaningful and useful. Those ideas do not always do well in traditional reliability testing, but it is incredible if you invite the leadership into the co-creation sessions. They get the perspective, they see the validity of the idea, and they are willing to lean in. Then the data delivers on the other side in the results once launched. I've seen that time and time again.

When I was the Olay brand manager for the skin care line, Olay was priced at $6 and it was incredibly cheap. Marketing wanted to charge $9.99 which would be a huge upcharge, but the pricing would have limited the investment in the product experience. I said, "Why would we charge that? People love this product. We should charge $29.99 and give them the right experience." And they said, "We can't do that. It is Olay." And so I said, "Why can't we? People love this product." Today, Olay sells in the US for $59.99, as more and more premium product initiatives have launched. Sometimes on these ideas, they have to be brought down to a person. You engage with a person who most likely you want to serve, and that is when you get your fresh perspective. They cannot tell you what they need. Steve Jobs used to say, "No one ever would have asked for an iPhone." But if you show them an iPhone mockup, they'll react to it and tell you what else they need. That is the idea of co-creation, to get a fresh perspective. Take something to them and then go from there. You get them on a level playing field, and then you can create. That is what I think is powerful – a powerful way to validate a new idea. Just do not keep it to yourself too long. Get out there with people who will bounce it around and build it. Time and time again, it works. It is amazing.

Here is another example. I recently worked with a professional B2B company, and they were trying to get engagement with their millennial practitioners. They were putting together a new marketing plan for an audience and we co-created for the first time. This company had never done that. But we took the ideas to the people they were trying to serve. The first marketing thing they put out post co-creation got about three times the response rate of anything they had ever done before. Why? Because it had been validated through the perspective of the user, of the person they were serving, the person they were trying to delight. We had the clarity of where we were headed, and what was meaningful and useful, and then when we went to launch this new B2B program, it got incredible engagement. They said, "What happened? We've never seen numbers like this before." We had built it with the user. We had not just built it to our own specifications. Now, in everything they do, they co-create.

It is also nice to have another set of eyes which don't know anything about the project. I sometimes will go to someone who disagrees with my philosophy in life or has a different point of view on a project just to get their counterpoint, because that fresh perspective is valuable too. That perspective helps you see the holes in your thinking – the holes that you cannot see because you are too close to it. I am not beyond talking to the person who disagrees with me.

My favorite place to get fresh perspective, however, is the co-creation side of things, because that is when you can get perspectives to validate your idea. The others help build your thinking, like a counter point of view. They help you strengthen your thinking and make sure there are no holes in it, but the co-creator validates the idea when you're co-creating with the user. That is my take on it. To do it well and to have it actually have some merit in decision making, you have to have the decision maker in the co-creation session. Because BASES, or whatever a team uses to evaluate an idea, will not always pick up the meaningful and useful nuances. When you're talking to design thinkers, you're getting co-creation.

What is the most important thing(s) that organizations need to change in order to be more open to new ideas or approaches?

This is really challenging. To me, the single biggest issue that I have seen, both at P&G and in the many other organizations that I have been working within the past six years, is the measurement system. Most types of operating measurement systems tend to provide incentives to maintain the system – to optimize it but not to innovate it. The most important thing, if you are running daily operations, is standardization, increasing utilization, and optimizing the use of resources. It is all about efficiency and effectiveness. These are the measures that business uses. Innovation inherently hurts all those measures.

The way that manufacturing works is to try to be at 85 to 90% of utilization of the machine, because you need 10 to 15% for updates, cleaning, and mainte-nance. All the things that need to be done to keep the machine running might drive utilization down to, for example, 85%. When you want to launch a new product, and you want to get test products, you have to slow the machine down to make something different, and so the utilization numbers go further down, to 80%. That is worth millions of dollars in efficiency. Organizations have to think about the metrics they use.

The way that I worked around this in my career was to try to create separate organizations. I divided businesses into groups of people that ran the business, and people who invented for the business, because you needed to run them through separate deliverables and separate metrics. You cannot do that in a sys-tem that is one-size-fits-all. The most important thing is having separate organi-zations. Someone who is creating something new needs time to explore the ideas that a team comes up with.

But the metrics for innovation are different from the metrics for optimi-zation. The leader of the business has to be able to hold both of those things simultaneously.

For example, after the Gillette acquisition, Ed Shirley had run beauty care for a number of years. He was the vice chair and wanted to improve the way the organization worked. I was involved in an effort on the P&G Prestige business, its fine fragrance business, to improve the business and morale. We wanted to try some new approaches – to help them create a coherent culture, where inno-vation flourished. We worked with that team for a year and a half. As we were developing our approach, we suggested to Ed, "You shouldn't hold the president accountable for his profit forecast this year. You have to give him a profit relief to make this organizational investment." He may feel doing these things might make it tough to deliver his profit commitment – he needs to realize that if he misses his forecast, he is not going to lose his job. Because you want him to create a culture of innovation. So you need to incentivize him to invest in a culture of innovation. Eventually, he took his profit forecast down so the business had the freedom to try a new approach.

The Prestige President was all on board with the profit relief, and he was enthusiastic, "Yeah, we are going for it. We are going to go for a culture of inno-vation." So we did it. We did the work. We got incredible results. Not only a great new pipeline but employee satisfaction results. Employee satisfaction went through the roof because it is a lot more fun to work in a culture of innovation. The work was absolutely amazing and the rest of the story is that they exceeded their profit forecast dramatically rather than needing the profit relief that year.

Not only did they make their profit, they exceeded their original forecast. We got there by giving them relief from the metrics of optimization. To me, the most important thing is the metrics and the way that you manage innovation vs optimization. In this case, it was a combo organization, they were doing both innovation business and optimization business. By giving them relief from a key metric, they had some degrees of freedom to make some bets.

By changing the metrics, you got people to focus on the human part of things.

One of the things I think that design thinkers miss in the practice of design thinking is the culture component. People talk about a culture of innovation, but they do not actually create the environment in which it can flourish. They just get in to do design thinking activities. Design thinking is fun, and people like to do it, but it does not sustain, because there is no culture to receive it.

The Prestige work is one of the things I am most proud of in the practice of design thinking at P&G. It was created with a lot of help from a lot of people – my key Prestige partner, David Kuehler, who led the Clay Street Project,[7] and Mukara Meredith of Matrix Works. At P&G, we invested in the human element of the group dynamic, and not just the idea dynamic. I took this approach to Stanford, and suggested to them, "You are missing the cultural component in your practice." At P&G, we dubbed this focus as social artistry, the social artistry of getting a group to be in relation to one another so that they can be creative.

I was really proud of what we did at P&G, and I took it to Stanford because I thought they could build it into their practice, but they were not that interested. I'll be honest; they're more interested in the ideas, and the fun, cool tools for ideating, and the cool tools for observing. And that is good. Those things are important, and that is their gift to the world. I have not seen them as interested in the ecosystem of the people in the room. If we are studying the human, we have to also have the humans in the room that are doing that studying, that are going out into that world, in relation to one another in a way to speak freely, be candid, disagree.

There is a great book called *High Commitment High Performance: How to Build A Resilient Organization for Sustained Advantage* by Michael Beer who was a Harvard Business School organizational design professor.[8] When we were doing this work with fine fragrance, David and I met with Beer to talk about what we were doing, because we found Beer's understanding of how to create candor in an organization helpful – candor is essential to innovation. If you do not have candor in an organization, then people will not share their wisdom, their ideas, and their concerns. All of that gets swept under the rug, and you miss something important. Either you miss the upside of the idea, or you miss a flaw in your thinking. I've seen this time and time again. You have to have candor.

What do you have to create, that creates creativity and innovation? Candor. But first, you have to establish safety in the room. If I disagree with you, I have to believe you are not going to fire me, even though you're three levels higher than I am in the organization. I need to be able to speak truth to power. That is the ultimate testament of candor. I mean I can be candid with my co-worker, but can I be candid with my CEO? If you cannot be, and you get punished, you certainly won't be candid.

I was punished once.

Here is the story. I was the brand manager on Pampers, and we were launching a major new product. I knew that product supply manufacturing was having trouble running at line speeds for my new product. It was a training pant, and every seventh pant did not seam correctly so that when the child went to pull it on it split open. I knew that mums carry one pant with them when they go out for a play date, a park or to the store. They do not carry a box of them. I knew that one failure is a complete failure. They have to go home. I had been fighting with product supply on this to make it clear to the president, who was going to sign off on the national launch, that we were not ready for a national launch, and they forbade me to say anything in the upcoming meeting with the Baby Care president. The president and I had a very good relationship. We had worked together over the years, and he trusted me, and I trusted him. So I am in this room of 20–25 people, most of whom were white males. Three women. This was the early 1990s. I am the lowest ranking person in the room. I am the brand manager, but there are all the powerful senior leaders at the meeting, because this was $100-million-dollar decision.

I am sitting in the back, outside of the group at the conference table. I am there "in case I am needed" by the advertising leader. The president looks around the room, and he is about to sign the paper. He goes, "We are ready to go then? We are ready to take on the training pant market?" And everyone is like, "We are ready. We are running at line speeds. We've got a BASES winner." He looks over at me, and he says, "So we're ready?" and I say, "Actually, no." I spoke truth to power. I was punished for months. People disagreed with me in the meeting. They told me I didn't know what I was talking about, and they told the president I didn't know what I was talking about. I said, "Every seventh side seam splits open. Imagine if they are at a family wedding and the one training pant they have splits open. So we are not ready. I do not have confidence that we are ready." And they all said, "She does not know what she is talking about. She is the marketer," and so they dismissed it. He signed the paper, and we lost millions of dollars on this decision because every seventh side seam split open. Mothers were angry. Mums felt that they had been betrayed. Walmart delisted us. It was just a horrible sequence of events.

I was on everyone's bad list for several months leading up to the launch, and no one would talk to me. I was put through all kinds of hoops. But it did play out the way that I said, and pretty much everyone who lied to him got fired or reassigned. I did not get fired. My point is the importance of speaking the truth, and I had spoken to all the players in the room beforehand about my concerns. We actually failed faster than usual because we had such a great trial plan. The marketing plan over-delivered on year one trial so we failed faster than we would have naturally because we had good marketing. As Michael Beer talks about in his book, if you do not have truth to power, if you do not have the ability to speak, leaders cannot make an informed decision.

If you do not have that basic ingredient in the room when you are creating, you will never get a good idea. Because people will edit themselves, "Oh, I do not know. This is risky, I am not going to say that it is not worth it. It is not worth the public humiliation to say this." So that is why I think creativity and innovation only really happen when people are free. They have to be free to explore, free to think, free to disagree, free to engage in discourse. When you do not have that, you get dysfunctional organizations, and you do not get innovation. By the time we finished with the Prestige business, where they did not have candor when we arrived, we had created an infrastructure to nurture it. We had people in the business at all levels elect people they wanted to represent their truth. And once a month, these six individuals from different parts of the organization would go to the leadership team meeting. The last hour of the leadership team meeting was for the people of the organization – from the manufacturing plant, from the marketing organization, etc. – to talk about how decisions being made by the leadership group were actually impacting them, how things that were being ignored by the leadership group were actually the big issues, and how opportunities that could have been capitalized on were not. We called that the ambassador team. They were the ambassadors of truth, elected by their peers, to go to the leadership team meeting, to speak truth to power, and there would be no negative ramifications for speaking truth in a productive way.

The leadership team would engage, and sometimes they would still continue to do what they were doing because of other factors. You make a decision, and you are aware of the consequences, but you are going to do it anyway. However, if you are aware of the consequences, then you can develop a mitigation plan for these consequences. Decisions did not always go the way people wanted. But they were informed, and this created an environment where people could come up with an idea and share it, where their morale went up and they had the environment that launched their most successful initiative.

If you do not have the freedom to speak and express yourself, you cannot innovate in an organization.

Notes

1 In the world of consumer-packaged goods, the term Desired Consumer Experience (DCE) is a synthesis of a consumer understanding of values and aspirations along with the product category's standards of excellence. DCE can provide multiple levels of understanding for the consumer-facing part of the organization. See https://thoughtleadership.yourencore.com/your-encore-consumer-goods-blog/key-elements-of-a-desired-consumer-experience-dce-2.

2 Standards of Excellence are often described in the Letters to Shareholders. See, for example: https://news.pg.com/press-release/pg-corporate-announcements/pg-highlights-significant-value-creation-progress-letter-sh.

3 A. G. Lafley led P&G from 2000 to 2010 and then again from 2013 to 2015, when he served as Chairman, President, and CEO. He discusses his strategy approach in Lafley, A. G., & Martin, R. L. (2013). *Playing to Win: How Strategy Really Works.* Boston, MA: Harvard Business Press.

4 See https://www.businesswire.com/news/home/20060809005051/en/Procter-Gamble-Chooses-BASES-Preferred-Global-Supplier.

5 Martin, R. (2009). *The Design of Business: Why Design Thinking is the Next Competitive Advantage*. Boston, MA: Harvard Business School Press.

6 Cindy discusses her view on user understanding and empathy in this article, where she also distinguishes between design research and market research. Tripp, C. (2013). No empathy –No service. *Design Management Review, 24*(3), 58–64. Available at: https://onlinelibrary.wiley.com/doi/pdf/10.1111/drev.10253.

7 Founded in 2004, the Clay Street Project is located a few blocks from P&G's General Offices in a remodeled industrial building in the heart of Over-the-Rhine, an urban renaissance area of Cincinnati. Being removed from the P&G environment encourages a shift in thinking and provides a buffer from the daily pressures of the business. Business teams can choose from different experiences based on their needs, ranging from 1–3 week experiences to more immersive 2–3 month sessions. For more information, see https://www.pg.com/en_US/downloads/innovation/factsheet_ClayStreet_FINAL.pdf.

8 Beer, M. (2009). *High Commitment, High Performance: How to Build a Resilient Organization for Sustained Advantage*. San Francisco, CA: Jossey-Bass.

17

VICTORIA VALLSTRÖM (BASTIDE)

When you put guardrails around your work and require outcomes that have to prove something, or it has to be very orderly and predictable, then you're not going to get an environment that is able to blossom creative innovation.

Victoria Vallström (Bastide) is the Chief Technical Officer at Lifesum, which is a Stockholm-based digital health company helping over 30 million users across the globe to achieve a healthier lifestyle. Using tech and psychology, Lifesum creates a tailored plan to help people live happier, more balanced lives.

Victoria's tech career began in Silicon Valley. After completing her computer science degree at San Jose State University, she started her professional career working for a computer software company called VMware. When Victoria was hired by VMware there was only a small team of 70 people, which rapidly grew to over 10,000. At VMware, Victoria was part of the engineering teams working on the VMware "kernel testing"; this included all the testing of CPU, memory, networking, and storage implementation of actual virtualization technologies (hypervisor).

After spending over ten years at VMware, Victoria then spent time working for niche companies such as Fusion-io and Virtual Instruments. Her time at Fusion-io was focused on caching software on flash card devices on servers to optimize read and write times toward large-scale computing. At Virtual Instruments, Victoria spent her time on a product to monitor storage area networks in real time. Then after 16 years in the US, Victoria returned to Sweden in 2014, where she decided that she wanted to do something different in the tech stack. Having always worked within an engineering organization that was very niche- and enterprise-driven, Victoria decided to move to the consumer side. She spent nearly two years working for Swedish Television (SVT), in which her team worked in backend services doing a majority of their Content Management

System (CMS) programs for SVTs' news sites and streaming services. And then about three years ago, Victoria joined Lifesum as the CTO. Her goals at Lifesum include working to enable the engineering teams to be the best that they can be, as she loves to create passionate, creative, innovative, and intrinsically motivated teams.

What is innovation to you?

When I think about innovative ideas, I think about two things. First, I view innovative ideas as cumulative. They do not come from a genius who comes up with a grand idea – and this might be different from other peoples' point of view – but I think that usually, they are cumulative and because they're cumulative they build on each other. Since they build on each other, the second view is that innovative ideas are usually in hindsight. So, in hindsight, you can say, "Yeah! That was really innovative."

I usually see innovative ideas emerge in response to a frustration or a need. There is always something that triggers innovative ideas, and many times I see them happen in front of me with a combination of deep knowledge coupled with some sort of naïve unawareness. When you put these two things together, that's usually when you are able to get these kinds of strange leaps. This is because you not only have a deep understanding of how something works but then on top of that you have someone that is open or naïve, and you are able to ask "Why can't we use this deep knowledge to do X or Y?" The VMotion feature at VMware is a perfect example of this being put into place. VMotion is the concept that you can live migrate a virtual machine between different servers. When it started around 2003, it was basically moving from one server to another. Then it became a 'disaster recovery' concept such as, "I lost this, I can move it over," and even then you had to have shared storage. There was a lot of different frames around it, and then if you look over time at how that developed, its focus shifted to live migrations, so it could be used across the globe, and you even started to use it for resource management. Instead of saying "if something fails, we migrate it," it became, "let's treat all of these hundreds of servers as a pool of resources and let these virtual machines autonomously move around." This idea is a huge foundation of cloud computing, which all started with VMotion.

The story behind how VMotion started I remember as this – one of our project managers who lost his laptop got extremely frustrated and said, "This is so funny. Here, sitting at this company, we know how to virtualize servers and have virtual machines running on them and I lose my whole system with a laptop. Why don't we use this technology to somehow take advantage of what we know? My laptop has a virtual machine on it." We already had the deep knowledge in place of how everything worked, such as how to deal with memory, CPU, disk, and the states of the different virtual machines. All we needed was how to complete the combination, and then VMotion came out. At the time, I remembered it as an idea surrounded by a lot of different ideas – there were none of us that thought, "That is the craziest most innovative thing ever." It was more like, "Okay, this is an interesting idea," but there were a lot of other neat things happening at the same time. Now, when we go back and look at how innovative and industry-changing it became, that is when we are able to realize and say "Wow, that was definitely the defining moment of VMware as a company," but we could not see it then, or I, at least, could not see it then, but you definitely see it afterwards.

I have another example of this concept from Lifesum. We have a very deep knowledge of design and our CPO (Chief Product Officer), Peter, comes from the advertising world. He actually doesn't have a deep tech background, so to him everything is centered on how the product looks and feels. We tried to solve this problem that when you use our product, you have to track everything that you're doing and when you track it, it takes quite a bit of time for us to get insights about the customer and how we can help improve their experience. We then thought we could get a head start by implementing a survey so the user can self-report issues they're having right when they happen.

There is a lot of research on the Healthy Eating Index (HEI), which essentially states what is healthy eating, how you can define it, and then get feedback. We designed 43 questions for our survey around HEI research and people said, "You guys are crazy. No one is going to take a 43-question survey." But then our CPO Peter said, "Well, let's try." He then designed the survey in a completely different way from how you would imagine a survey would be, and it included several pictures without a lot of text. People actually enjoyed answering the survey, and during the first two months we had over two million people completing all 43 of these questions. That is more than the majority of people using our app. It was almost like this openness, which we encouraged with our naïveté in making the survey so enjoyable for respondents, created a wealth of information that overwhelmed us. We couldn't initially say, "That was a great idea," because it took nearly an entire year for us to step back and think, "There's a lot of people taking this survey. I wonder why."

We now have a separate team here dedicated to working on the health test. From there we started to connect with universities; for example, we are working with Harvard University on nutrition. Specifically, taking their deep knowledge of science and nutrition and then marrying it with our way of using design in a different way. It has been two years since we launched our health test survey, and we are now working with Harvard on their own Alternative Healthy Eating Index research and how we can incorporate that into our Lifesum product. Again this is all cumulative, but if we look back now we can say, "It was so obvious, why did not we realize it then?" This is because innovative ideas take time to develop.

To me, these are the best examples of innovative ideas. I look at it as being aware that they are usually not from some mastermind that comes up with an innovative idea and everyone immediately knows it is "the one" – I have actually very rarely seen that in my own experience. This is why I believe that when we try too hard to find innovative ideas, we suffocate creativity.

How do you create an environment/culture that enables creativity and innovation?

I think we are in love with this idea of having a talented genius coming up with a brilliant, creative idea because we love that story. It is because this story sounds so much more fun than the process that takes a long time and you maybe do not understand until hindsight what you actually created. The most important mechanism becomes how to build an environment for creating all of these innovative ideas, foster them, and then have the right circumstances where people can make these connections from deep knowledge to naïve openness. The most important job I feel I have is to create such an environment, and that's essentially why I go to work every day.

My foundation principle is the idea of how you view a human being and then how you view talent. Many people think about talent as searching for this person with an innate talent and then you include them and that's going to make things go well. I view talent as being widely distributed and either suppressed or amplified by environment. A majority of it goes into how you view people, and then how you set up the best environment for them based on that view.

One of the things that we work a lot on at Lifesum is figuring out what the key elements are to set up an environment for creative innovation. For us, we look at three things. We look at collaboration, diversity, and unstructured work. Those are the three pillars that we work on. Working in a team and collaborating trumps competition and trying to pit people against one another. This is why we always view everything as a team effort. It is not your idea versus my idea, it is our idea together and then figuring out how we can improve together.[1] Everything we design here, we design from team goals. Although a person might want to have individual progression when they feel that they are developing, we try to do this as a team. When we hire into a team, we create what we call situational teams. I like the term situational teams because I think a lot of people talk about situational management.[2] Different teams need different things. When you allow people to be who they are, usually it turns out for the better because you amplify the good things. One team might be composed of a different set of people. When we hire a backend developer, some might need a different profile than for another team because they need to fit into that team and that environment, not necessarily be a cookie-cutter description for a certain type of person.

The second pillar is diversity. Here, we say diversity is "working with someone not like you." We have obvious measures like gender diversity, nationality diversity, and age diversity because they're easy to measure. We also realize that there are different diversity measures such as introvert and extrovert and socioeconomic background; it really can be all kinds of things. We are 54 people with 21 unique nationalities. We have a gender split of 44% female and 56% male, which is a phenomenal gender split for a tech company. In the age category, we tend to be a younger company, as we are roughly 75% below 35. We really try to have an environment of diversity at Lifesum. We say that it is important to understand that we're not simply emphasizing diversity in the workplace because it is the politically correct thing to do but because it's actually the best way to give you a diverse set of unique ideas. This opens up lots of different perspectives, and this is how you are able to create an environment where you have more opportunities to find things.

We talk a lot about diversity too because I think often people forget that diversity is damn hard. People think, "Okay, we have a diverse team," and then everything else will naturally fall into place, and this is not always true. There is a study about this concept that I like to talk about a lot within the company as well as when we first hire people.[3] The study involved observing three different groups who are trying to solve a murder mystery. In the first group, everyone knows each other, then there is another group in which only two people know each other, and finally there is a diverse group of people who do not know each other at all. The study has found a way to measure who is most successful at solving the murder mystery, and the results it shows are not surprising, as the diverse team outperforms the non-diverse teams. However, the really interesting part about the study is when they go back and ask the teams how they think they performed; the diverse team will usually say, "Oh, this was terrible. It did not go well at all," and then the very homogeneous team will confidently state, "We nailed it. It went really well." I like to use this example to show people and help them realize that sometimes it might not feel like it's good, but it is good.

The final pillar is unstructured work. It is not binary that everything is unstructured. However, when you put guardrails around your work and require outcomes that have to prove something or it has to be very orderly and predictable, then you are not going to get an environment that is able to blossom creative innovation. You have to accept how things are – they are not predictable. There is a lot of uncertainty and you might have a lot of failures. And then eventually something might come out of it. I sometimes deal with resistance to this unstructured approach because people want a lot of structure and certainty. It can be the board, other parts of leadership, or even team members who say, "Why don't we have the data for everything right now? Why don't we know this right now?," but I think that hinders a lot of the creative and innovative ideas from blossoming.

Unstructured work does not necessarily mean that there is no process involved at all, as there is definitely a process. However, it is more about having the understanding that when you are dealing with uncertainty, you cannot analyze and predict. You have to probe and react, and that is a little bit more unstructured. I do not always have all the answers, I cannot say to you, for example, "Let's come up with 15 innovative ideas and one out of these 15 will be great." I can't predict that. I do not know that. An example of an unstructured process we have at Lifesum is that we have two weeks a year where we let everyone do whatever they want with no restrictions on it. It's structured in the sense that we give people a certain amount of time to do whatever they want. If it means they want to clean their inbox or create something really crazy for the product, then they can do that. We do this once in the fall and once in the spring and it's produced some great results. Our photo recognition, for example, came out of this experience. I think this is because often the teams have a lot of knowledge and they have the itch to do something with it. I am conflicted about it just because sometimes this process can feel forced, but in the end it is good because it allows people to feel like it is okay to experiment. We want people to think through what kind of work they are trying to do and then we get out of the way so they can work with whoever they want and whenever they want during those two weeks.

One of the things that we do in those two weeks is to organize a breakfast each morning, where each nationality has the opportunity to cook for the rest of the teams. We do a lot of these things just to kind of put some structure in place. Everyone meets in the morning. Then we have some talks at lunch that can be about specific topics, and we invite interesting guest speakers. And then there is a big (product) demo at the end of each week. According to Peter, if you change some of your normal habits the week before the two unstructured weeks, you actually open your mind a little bit and therefore we can do more fun things. Like you could eat different breakfasts the week before. Take a different route to work. Doing a lot of different things to kind of prepare them for the two weeks ahead.[4]

The most important part to think about throughout the year is to figure out what you should continuously do to enable teams to constantly think about other ways to solve problems. It is a cliché, but the hardest thing is establishing psychological safety for the team and building trust, because you do not dare to experiment and go out on a limb if you know that you are going to be either punished or reevaluated for it. If you tell someone, "I'm only going to let you do this if you can prove to me that this is going to have this outcome," then you are not going to be able to build trust. You have to be okay with the fact that you might not always have an outcome.

What is the most important thing(s) that organizations need to change in order to be more open to new ideas or approaches?

I think the first thing organizations should do is to structure what they are doing in order to know where they want to have innovative ideas and creativity. If we say that we want to be a creative and innovative company, then it all depends – certain areas make more sense to approach creatively and innovatively. It is not all or nothing. You need to determine where you want to be creative and innovative, and then also be able to say, "No, we're fine with where we are here." This ties back to being open to a diversity of ideas, but to be open is not always easy because diversity is hard. If you are in a heated debate about something, you understand it's not about people but it's about having different perspectives. And that also goes back to trust. If you have trust, you can have a very positive conflict of ideas. If you have the trust, then these debates can become extremely productive. Having a diversity of ideas is one of the best things that a company can do.

Organizations also need to show an openness and patience that not every-thing needs to show results immediately in the area(s) where they want to have innovation. It is a leap of faith that the organization has to commit to, and that is especially hard for a VC-backed company like us. It is a lot easier said than done, because so many things are pulling at you. There always will be this sense of fric-tion, but identifying some key areas is helpful. Our health test for example – we took a strategic shift this fall before we had the whole company working on the Lifesum product. We did this because of what we saw with the health test, and we started to think if we take the scientific approach together with our design, it would work because we've seen this work before. We basically parsed out a team that was completely on their own, and they could do whatever they wanted within that realm. We tried to make sure that they could operate without too many points of coordination with the rest of us. That's where we want them to be so they can be innovative. This is also how we could get the board's support because we say, "Okay, here is where we're going to do this and here is how we're going to fund that project." It's extremely important to know where you want to be innovative and know where you want to keep on going along with what is working for you.

We talk a lot about teams and not superstars at Lifesum. Always having the mindset that it is not my idea, it is our idea. We think together, and we build together. There is also a misconception sometimes that when you are a team and working together that you need to be aware of not taking up space. I sometimes joke that this is the American in me, but I make sure to tell teams, "Don't be afraid to stand out and be a total kick ass on something. Be proud of it, show it, and take up space." This is completely fine, as long as you don't do it to the detri-ment of others and you bring people with you along the way.

Who do you generally approach to get a fresh perspective on an idea or otherwise to validate an idea?

Whenever I need a fresh perspective on what I am working on, I go to our CPO Peter, because it's been so interesting to work with him. I have had a lot of peers throughout my career, and I would say Peter and I are the most differ-ent from each other than anyone else I have ever worked with. He comes from advertising, whereas I come from the world of enterprise tech. Peter is extremely open, unstructured, the "classic creative." He has a completely different way of approaching things from me. We are like yin and yang. But during these past two-and-a-half years, we have really established a way to work with each other. I help him with some of his weaknesses around structuring things, and he helps me in the areas where I have my weaknesses, usually about thinking wider and differently, without making me feel like he is intruding or tearing down my ideas. Peter has this way – when you walk into a room with him and talk about an idea, you always walk out with a better idea than when you came in. The way he helps me polish and refresh my ideas reminds me of improv theatre. One of the ground rules of improv theatre is that you can never block, and by that I mean when someone does something, you have to follow along with it. If you take an opposite approach to what someone else is doing, it is called blocking because you kill the scene. And you would be surprised how hard that is, not blocking in improv, it was eye opening to me and a great learning experience. I feel like this is very similar to working with other people. If you come up with an idea and someone just tried to shoot it down, you're basically blocking them instead of saying, "Interesting, so how about this, and how about this?" and then you can morph those ideas together. When you are able to take your original idea and then morph it into another idea, it makes you feel like you are part of the process. Peter is phenomenal at that. If it's regarding people, product, tech, and so on, it's always great to go to him with an idea in mind.

Do you have any beliefs about innovation that might not necessarily be held by others?

This ties back to my definition of innovation, and it is the common idea of the genius who comes up with the innovative idea that changes a company. I do not necessarily believe in having a brainstorming session or an innovation week because I feel like it puts too much pressure on thinking that you're going to come up with an amazing new idea that will put you ahead of competitors. I'm much more centered on realizing that it's a long process and when you do eventually arrive at realizing it was an innovative idea, it's usually long after the fact. It's more about being open to the fact that you might have multiple ideas going at once and you need to nurture them in the hope that one of them becomes a great idea.

My beliefs about innovative ideas go hand in hand, again, with my beliefs on how you view talent. Anyone has the capability, and some people might have more outward-looking talent, like Peter, for example. He is extensively creative, but maybe that is a direct result of the process of his spending 25 years in an advertising agency. Is it cause or effect? I think it's having the foundation principle that everyone has the talent. It is then up to you what you do to amplify or suppress that talent. That's not always the main trend, I would say, in ideas. Some people that come here to Lifesum sometimes think we seem a little too nice, not as aggressive as we should be. They ask, "Why don't we talk more about the individual, etc.?" I have encountered some scepticism over our setup, but I do not think these critics realize that the setup at Lifesum is very intentional.

How do you help people accept failure?

I can give you an example of how we frame decisions and failures and let people understand why we have this philosophy and where we go from there.

The Cynefin framework has been really useful both for me and I think for others because it is a way to look at how you work and make decisions. It is composed of four different sections; *complex, complicated, chaotic,* and *simple.*

Something is *simple* when the obvious things like cause and effect relationships exist because they are predictable and repeatable. They function to help you sense, categorize, and respond because that usually results in best practice. If someone starts here at Lifesum, they have 15 accounts that they need to be added to, for example. That is very similar to the Cynefin model. So then, if we don't have to be unstructured and we can operate within this system, we can achieve best practice.

Sometimes things are *complicated* when the relationship between cause and effect exists but isn't as self-evident as you require. So you analyze it, investigate, and then you usually have to have a domain expert that knows how to do it. You need to sense, analyze, and then respond; that is usually when you have best practice in place.

Then there is the *complex* where the cause and effect is only obvious with hindsight. Unpredictable outcomes emerge. You conduct falsifiable experiments, and then you amplify and adjust depending on what you are seeing so you can probe, sense, and respond. This is an emergent practice, and it is a new way of doing things.

Then you also have *chaos,* which you can easily fall into. But the interesting thing about this is that we use this state as a structure for how people should think.

Most of the time, we all feel like we are in the "middle" – we do not know what type of situation we are in. And then we tend to choose the problem solving technique we are most comfortable with, the context in which we have mostly worked. For example, if you are used to a predictable and simple environment, you tend to view the world through that lens. Then you get extremely frustrated when you work with someone else with a different perspective and background. This framework helps people navigate through the types of scenarios and problems. And then when you start approaching the complex areas, it is much easier to articulate and understand, so tolerance for failure, uncertainty, risk, and experimentation grows. When you move into complex areas, failure will happen – as you don't have access to predictable cause and effect.

Notes

1 Equality and team rather than individual is very much part of the Scandinavian culture, which raises questions about how to adapt any of the teaching on innovation to the specific cultural context in which they are implemented. To learn more about this we recommend starting with the work of the Happiness Research Institute and the books written by its CEO, Meik Wiking. Wiking, M. (2016). *The Little Book of Hygge: The Danish Way to Live Well.* London, UK: Penguin Random House. See also www.happinessresearchinstitute.com.

2 Situational management and situational leadership have been developed over the years by Paul Hersey and Ken Blanchard in the 1970s. The key idea behind the approach is that there is no single "best" style of leadership. Effective leadership should consider the task at hand and effective leaders should adapt the leadership style to the individual or team they are attempting to influence and the goal that

needs to be accomplished. See Hersey, P., & Blanchard, K. H. (1979). *Management of Organizational Behavior.* Englewood Cliffs, NJ: Prentice Hall.

3 You can read about the original study in Phillips, K. W., Liljenquist, K. A., & Neale, M. A. (2009). Is the pain worth the gain? The advantages and liabilities of agreeing with socially distinct newcomers. *Personality and Social Psychology Bulletin, 35*(3), 336–350.

4 This is a rather interesting approach. An example is a large US firm that, before a big decision, sent its company executives to activities such as skiing. The rationale was that dealing with risk in a setting like sports would help executives deal with risky decisions at work.

18

STEFAN VLACHOS

Over time, I have realized that in order to have immediate impact on what happens, you have to work with what you have at hand, and then you can think about further what goes on afterwards.

Stefan Vlachos is the Head of the Center for Innovation at the Karolinska University Hospital, where he has worked for the past five years. He is responsible for innovation management, including strategy, methods, portfolio, and securing innovation partnerships with industry. Before his work at Karolinska University Hospital, Stefan spent 20 years working in the private sector, including the telecommunication, internet, media, entertainment, and energy industries.

Stefan is an engineer by training. It was not until receiving an MBA from INSEAD that Stefan realized he was more passionate about the uses of technology than its development. This was the beginning of Stefan's innovation journey, and his ideas are now centered around the adaptive applications of existing and new technologies.

What is innovation to you?

In my view, it is quite innovative to actually think inside the box, and work with what you have.

When I started my professional career, I had this great idea that technology would be the only tool used in solving problems. Over time, I've realized that in order to have an immediate impact on what happens, you have to work with what you have at hand, and then you can think about what goes on afterwards. For example, at Karolinska, we were working with heart failure patients who were often returning to the ER immediately after discharge. One of the key solutions we implemented was setting up a specialized office that included a small team of highly experienced nurses and doctors who would receive phone calls from discharged patients who had questions or concerns. The phone line was staffed at normal office hours only, but it was still able to increase the feeling of security for these patients enormously, and it led to a 50% reduction in the number of repeat visits to the ER. That is quite a radical change from such a simple solution. We were able to increase the quality of care for these patients at a very low cost. In this situation, a way of creative thinking was actually thinking inside the box with what we had available.

Do you have an example of something people consider to be innovative, but you don't?

I am not very fond of odd gadgets. Having spent five years in the medical field, there is a lot of gadget innovation surrounding the lower end of medical technology. For example, another dispenser for surgical gloves or a new way to take skin biopsies. These are considered innovations by many, but they are really more of a redesign; a very small incremental improvement, but not an innovation.

The idea of a simple redesign being considered innovation is not uncommon. For example, Apple's new product launches are touted by Apple as innovation but perhaps are not generally considered so by most people: "We made a gold colored iPhone." That is not innovation but a simple redesign of one of their products that was already on the market. Apple is great at bringing products together, but not at being the first. They are the first to make sense of things and put them into scale.

However, the app store, that was real innovation. I worked in the mobile industry for a number of years focusing on mobile gaming and mobile TV, and there were several different types of app stores in place for a long time. What Apple was able to do before anyone else was truly make the ecosystem work. I looked at the tech development funds over a period of seven years, and in this time period tech specifications (amount of memory, speed of the processors, bandwidth, etc.) increased by a factor of 25 to 60. But at the same time, the number of apps in the app store had increased 3,000 times. This was because the business models were not previously in place. The technical platforms did slightly improve, but the entire ecosystem and its working functions truly came into play when Apple launched its app store.

What is important to note here is that was an innovation of the business model rather than an innovative technology. I am very fond of business model innovation because it is much more satisfying to work on and it can have even more profound impacts within the organization. It is always aided by interaction between technology development and business model innovation; in other words for the whole solution, both business model innovation and technological innovation must work together.

Where do you find sources of inspiration for new ideas or opportunities?

I think that examining and experiencing a variety of things – especially as a beginner – is always stimulating, because your learning curve is so steep when you are a beginner. Beginning to learn something new opens up the ways to make associations.[1] I have worked in five or six different industries in a number of different countries, and that has led to a number of diverse experiences. In my free time I like to learn to do many different things, such as making bread, hunting, making sausages, skating, and reading because they create connections in different parts of my brain. Additionally, pop culture has been a major source of inspiration for me because it opens up the means to use imagination in generating innovative solutions.[2]

Association is probably one of the most important tools to have in your creative portfolio. By this, I mean the ability to associate "this works here," and "I saw that pattern there." This is extremely useful in all three innovation horizons;[3] which are working within what you have, associating the potential of your assets by using them in different ways, and then the ability to look further into the horizon and imagining what could be by stretching the potential of the solutions in front of me. For me, a great example of this is the evolution of video home rentals. I worked a lot in entertainment, and I was able to see in front of me what happened over a period of time. When I was growing up, I took my bike and rode down to the store to rent a movie box and a VHS cassette, and then I rode home again to watch the movie. This has completely changed over a period of 20 years or so, but in steps, and you can see how those steps were taken. I can also apply that to where I'm working now, in healthcare. Of course, healthcare is much more regulated than the video rental industry, but that's simply the boundary conditions that we work within that we are able to expand over time. This is one of the things I really appreciate about the people I work with: their ability to use their imagination. They are able to look at something and say, "What would that mean somewhere else?"

Most important for finding sources of inspiration is variety. I've always been a generalist in what I do. For example, I chose engineering physics to study at university because in the university handbook it said I would learn the timeless tools of mathematics, physics, etc. This meant that I would not be boxed into one skillset. If I had chosen to study to be a high-voltage electrical engineer, then it would have been very focused on high-voltage electrical engineering. And what if that specialty had eventually become irrelevant because someone else discovered something else? I wanted a generalistic way of looking at complex problems.[4] The ability to become a real expert in a very narrow field is important, but it's not for me.

Do you have any beliefs about innovation that might not necessarily be held by others?

There is a common, democratic notion that everyone can do innovation, and it's true that everyone can probably contribute in some way. However, the ability to contribute to radical and disruptive innovation is not for everyone. You have to have the stamina to endure lots of setbacks that include many highs and sometimes even more lows. You have to be able to cope with the idea that you do not know what is going to happen tomorrow. If it truly changes something fundamentally, then it's not going to be a fun ride all the time. Some people don't function well in these types of environments. For example, one of the first start-ups I joined in the late 1990s was a telecom start-up. This was around the time when telecoms were being deregulated in Sweden, so of course there was the old monopoly and a few other start-ups coming in. We started with very few people, but then we eventually started to grow and even brought in some people from the incumbent monopoly that had over 40,000 employees. They didn't like it, because we didn't have processes for everything. In fact, we had processes for almost nothing and made up most of it as we went along. If you spend a whole lifetime working in an environment where there's right and wrong, where there's always guidelines and policies, you will not thrive in an uncertain environment. Everyone can have great ideas and have good opinions, but to follow them through is completely different.

Businesses need to be innovative but at the same time get things done today, that is, they have a portfolio of opportunities to invest in for both the short and the long term. How should a business balance the short-term necessities and the long-term goals? What has been your personal experience in approaching this particular challenge?

One of the things that we are trying to do now is to look at a particular need, problem, or opportunity, and then see how we can phase that in different stages. For a short-term stage, we address this particular problem in the short term with what we have.[5] Then in parallel, either with the same group or a different group, we try to imagine what could be for this particular situation. For example, let's talk about waiting times in the ER. We could start out with simply making the process better, such as applying resources for triage by putting the most experienced doctors up front instead of in the back. Eventually, and maybe in the next step, we could try to implement an AI-assisted self-assessment. And finally, in the third stage, we try to use our imaginations for future solutions. One example might be, "We could all have chip implants that will record our current metabolism and body moves to detect up front if something is going to go wrong." Working on these three horizons in parallel, gives us quick wins and the momentum to move to other solutions over time.

We all have different abilities to offer in our work, and I haven't yet figured out if it should be the same or different teams that work to different horizons, because you have to have a variety of knowledge and different mindset for each problem. I once saw a lecture where someone said that "horizon three feeds the pipeline to horizon two, which feeds the pipeline to horizon one." This sums it up nicely, because what is considered horizon three will certainly become horizon one in five years. If you are able to frame your needs or problems in a semi-generic way, then you can adjust your horizons as needed over time. There will always be the outsiders who say, "Okay, let's completely disregard that need and definitely look at this one."[6]

Are there any managerial principles, techniques, processes, or other things that might be good in theory but haven't worked in practice in your experience?

Management is particularly important when it comes to innovation, but I don't think that there is a general answer to this. We can again relate this to the different horizons and the different ways to manage within the different horizons. For example, the CFO might be a very influential person in horizon one, but the CFO should definitely be kept away from horizon three. The management by Excel principle does not work in this case. I think that our hierarchical notions, where the responsibility for making decisions is at the top, are appropriate in certain environments. The principles of gathering facts and making informed choices based on the facts works well in a no-uncertainty environment. When you go out into a highly uncertain environment, then you have to break free from that. For people like me, managing a team of 20 – and I have very strong opinions at times – sometimes I have to step back and say, "What can we do to figure out the best way if we think according to A, B, or C?" You have to actually do something and provoke something in order to get the best basis for decisions, and that's also not very traditional.

I recently read something about the idea of the Chief Experimenting Officer instead of the Chief Executive Officer,[7] and that is much more inclusive. In that way, you have to really challenge the people who are supposed to do the experiments. This is a mindset not just from a management point of view but from most people's view about needing to work in certainty. Defining a project in stages feels comfortable to people. Defining an experiment and then saying at the outset what will be the success or otherwise of that experiment is really hard for some, so you have to push that success. There is a long-standing principle of management that I have found to be true no matter where I've been, and that's "Nag, nag, nag or repeat, repeat, repeat."

Do you believe that the team dedicated to innovations can be located in the same premises as someone like the CFO, or should they be separated from the rest of the organization? What are the boundaries? Is there a different model there?

I would say that it highly depends on both the industry and the organization. In our case, as a hospital, there are some fairly tight regulations that will prevent us from putting disruptive innovations in place. However, we are now thinking of how we can incubate or accelerate, to even bring an incubation or acceleration program type of thinking into a small dedicated part of the hospital. We haven't implemented it yet, because we have to consider all the ethical and patient safety implications. This also goes to defining what our measure of success is. Our measure of success is not growth. Our measure of success is essentially a healthier population, or even more specifically, curing a patient's disease.

But in a company it's different, and I would consider having a separate innovation space. I heard an interview with the head of electric cars from one of the big German car manufacturers, and they were asked, "What's your biggest hurdle?" It's not something in the market, it's the managers for petrol engines, because they go outside and create a new environment, some sort of creative destruction. Some companies have managed this kind of situation well, and others not.

Following that question, do you think that there is such a thing as a minimum viable product (MVP) for healthcare?

That process is in place in both MedTech and pharma and it is highly regulated. As we discussed earlier, much of the innovation in the kind of healthcare we provide today will be business model innovation. In that case, yes, I think MVPs can be done. The model that I described earlier with the heart failure patients can be seen as the MVP. It's not the wire frame type of product, but it's the setup where we can take two rooms, two nurses, a doctor, a couple of beds, and a phone. We then eventually added video conferencing capabilities and viability to look through the ER ledgers to see if there is someone there who probably has heart failure, based on the views of the highly experienced nurses and doctors. This will probably be done with a more digital tool later on, as this all requires a bit of imagination. How do we set up such a minimum viable way of working? This relates to designing your experiment, if you are talking lean enterprise, lean start-up ways. The experiment design way is tough because simply identifying your most crucial assumption and defining that experiment requires a lot of training.

Value chain analysis is quite important as well when we look at what value we provide to our patients or how we can help them. The patients and the professional staff are the two main constituents. Then, of course, there are the politicians and the other stakeholders, but they are secondary. If you consider them as primary, then you are on the wrong track.

How do you build a great narrative/story for a novel idea? Is there a formula?

There is a simple way to describe the formula – center it around the person or the group that actually benefits from whatever you're trying to accomplish and then take that as a starting point. What's the journey that you go through?[8] Journeys are very powerful, so illustrating them well and personalizing them, maybe with the use of a particular name, can improve your narrative. Obviously, talk about the concepts that you are working on, but then after that talk about what happened to get the narrative both of the winding road that you had to take and the individuals who influenced the decisions or the changes in direction. That becomes very powerful. Another ingredient that is particularly important in the hospital environment is to tell more than just one story. The doctor, nurse, and physiotherapist all have different stories. I can talk about small general things and applaud the people who work at the front line, but I shouldn't be the one who is telling the story.

If the story is told to an audience, then the follow-up questions become much deeper, or the answers are much deeper when answered by doctors, nurses, physiotherapists, etc., because they have firsthand experience.

We increasingly use video for storytelling in healthcare. Video is great for illustrating the problem, although not as good for presenting the idea. It helps the audience understand the problem and the storytelling can become quite powerful.

Notes

1 For the neuroscience of innovative ideas, see Berns, G. (2010). *Iconoclast: A Neuroscientist Reveals How to Think Differently*. Boston, MA: Harvard Business Press. One of the authors (Massimo) interviewed Matteo Berlucchi, the founder of Your. MD. Matteo made an interesting observation. Are you an insider or an outsider? If you are an insider, you understand the market, understand the deficiencies and the shortcomings, and come up with an idea to improve the system. If you are an outsider, you do not know how the system works from the inside, so you just look at it from the outside, and you think of ways to improve it for the end user, disregarding the dynamics of the internal system. Therefore, when you are stuck in understanding the value that is brought to the customer or how value can be delivered, it might be the time for you to engage with industry outsiders to bring that perspective. For more insights, see Garbuio, M., & Lin, N. (2019). Artificial Intelligence as a Growth Engine for Healthcare Start-ups: Emerging Business Models. *California Management Review*, 61(2), 59–83.

2 See McCracken, G. D. (2011). *Chief Culture Officer: How to Create a Living, Breathing Corporation*: Basic Books. If you want to learn more about using ethnography to run interviews, see McCracken, G. D. (1988). *The Long Interview* (Vol. 13). Newbury Park, CA: Sage.

3 See the Three Horizon framework in "Resources" in Part 3.

4 Compare with Jeanne Marell's interview.

5 Compare with Victoria Bastides's interview.

6 See the Three Horizon framework in "Resources" in Part 3.

7 See http://www.theinnovationscout.com/c-e-o-the-new-chief-experiments-officer-leads-innovation/.

8 Some excellent resources on journey mapping, or experience mapping, are Liedtka, J., & Ogilvie, T. (2011). *Designing for Growth: A Design Thinking Toolkit for Managers*. New York, NY: Columbia University Press; and Fraser, H. M. (2012). *Design Works: How to Tackle your Toughest Innovation Challenges through Business Design*. Toronto: University of Toronto Press.

19

MELISSA WIDNER

We are constantly inspired by the founders of start-ups. I was a start-up CEO before my role at NAB, and now I have the good fortune of spending time with visionary and creative people – on a regular basis.

Melissa Widner is a General Partner at NAB Ventures, a division of NAB, Australia's largest business bank. NAB Ventures is a global initiative supporting entrepreneurs in Australia and offshore in their quest to build leading technology companies. NAB is a market leader in business banking with specific focuses on SMEs, agriculture, health, and education. NAB Ventures invests in enterprises that can leverage the bank's expertise, assets, and market position to drive growth in investee companies.

Melissa has a strong understanding of both the entrepreneur's journey and the role of a venture capitalist. As co-founder and CEO of 7Software, a Silicon Valley enterprise software company, she oversaw its acquisition by Concur Technologies while providing over a tenfold return to investors. Melissa is also an active angel investor and served on the board of the US-based Alliance of Angels, one of the longest-running and most active angel groups in the world. In academic pursuits, she was a lecturer of venture capital and entrepreneurship at the University of Washington's MBA program, as well as a graduate of business and education at Stanford University. In Sydney, she co-founded Heads Over Heels, an organization that works with women entrepreneurs leading companies with high growth potential, and she currently serves on the board of AVCAL, the Australian Venture Capital Association.

What is innovation to you?

Innovation is such a commonly used word now. While other banks and big organizations have similar initiatives, NAB has been particularly innovative with its NAB Labs and NAB Ventures. The CEO created these to increase innovation and bring new ideas into the bank through closer collaboration with fintechs. It can be difficult for start-ups to collaborate with large established companies, as they are often unaware of the options available to them. One of the bank's goals in starting NAB Ventures and NAB Labs was to create a place where these start-ups and other potential partners from the fintech community could explore collaboration with the bank. At Ventures we help our portfolio companies, and sometimes companies that we do not invest in, to navigate the bank to optimize their journey. For example, a start-up may spend time meeting with different stakeholders, yet many of these meetings will not help them move forward for various reasons. We help navigate that journey.

NAB Labs was started as an innovation hub inside the bank to investigate new products and how they might work for our customers. NAB Labs works with external companies to test new ideas, giving us an opportunity to experiment and fail. Unlike business units, which are less able to devote resources to something that may not work, Labs can try many new ideas, knowing that probably only a few will work. Other banks have similar approaches. ANZ and Westpac have venture funds, although their approaches are different, with Westpac's external to the bank. It seems that venture funds may become a more common model for banks with an increase from two corporate venture funds in Australia in 2011 to 13 in 2018.[1]

There is no perfect model – different models work in different situations – and therefore types of venture funds vary according to their goal. While we hope Ventures brings a good financial return, it is not the reason for setting up the fund. Our goal is strategic more than financial. We want to bring innovation into the bank. With that as the goal, it is important to have the fund sit inside the organization, because one of the benefits that we bring to our companies is help navigating the organization.

Overall, an internal model works better for both strategic and financial goals because we are able to bring value to companies as a strategic partner.[2] We also take an approach that is unique for venture funds. Unlike most corporates, we will lead deals; that is, we will set the price and terms of a funding round. Some corporate venture funds require a business unit to sponsor a company before they make the investment. That can be difficult, because it has the potential to slow down the process, which may mean missing out on strategically significant opportunities. While it is important to have a clear idea of an investment's strategic importance or potential financial success, it is not a requirement to have a commercial partnership in place prior to making an investment.

Being truly disruptive is difficult. Innovation is more likely to be incremental than radical. This is the case for banks, as for any other organization. Banks in Australia compared to the US are quite far ahead in many areas. For example, most payments in Australia use tap technology. The NPP (New Payments Platform),[3] which launched in 2017, allows Australians to instantaneously pay others with simply their email address or mobile phone number. It allows, for instance, two people to have a coffee together and for one to reimburse the other instantly. In the US, tapping (for payments) is just starting to become prevalent. Another example is the use of cheques for payment. They are rarely used in Australia, unlike the US. Because Australia is a small market, it is easier to effect change and adopt it broadly, especially when all four banks are aligned. Innovation can sometimes happen faster in a smaller market.

Where do you find sources of inspiration for new ideas or opportunities?

At NAB, we are constantly inspired by the founders of start-ups. I enjoy spending time with visionary and creative people on a regular basis.

We do not follow a strict system when seeking new investment ideas. Some of the process relies on serendipity, but we are also very deliberate. Many of our investments have been made into companies that were not raising capital when we initially approached them.

We do a global market scan and focus on a few categories and geographies. We then look at what companies have good traction, founders, and investors. This process is quite deliberate, but serendipity comes into play through introductions from our networks inside and outside the bank. We meet with our investment committee, which consists of five senior leaders from NAB and one external venture capitalist, every three weeks. Much of our time is spent discussing the strategic benefits of investing in one company versus another. We have also created an advisory team made up of 30 leaders across the bank.

We have looked at over 2,000 companies since we started. We investigate and meet with companies, gradually refining our selections before we finally make the decision to invest. Interestingly, we have not made a single investment in a company that approached us cold, although we do consider them.

When you or your team have identified new ideas, how do you select the ones to pursue and the ones to discard? Is there an approach or a methodology?

Mostly we consult with others within the bank when making decisions to determine if there is partnership potential with a prospective investee.

How we select which companies to look at is very dependent on that individual business. We have to be able to clearly state how we can add value to the company beyond just the monetary investment. We also have to be able to answer the questions: "How will an investment in this company bring a better experience to our customers?" "How will it make the bank more efficient?" This is where our advisory team is invaluable. They will often refer us to others who can answer our questions. In a large organization, it is impossible to keep track of every initiative.

In venture, it helps to be a good networker externally, but in corporate venture, navigating the internal network is equally, if not more, important.

We do not pursue an incoming idea if we decide it is not strategic at that time or if we cannot prioritize it over other opportunities. Our portfolio right now is two-thirds Australian, one-third overseas, but more money is spent overseas because these companies tend to be in the later stages of development. Most of the companies I work with directly happen to be overseas because that is where my networks are, but these companies all have some plans for Australia.

What is the most important thing(s) that organizations need to change in order to be more open to new ideas or approaches?

Before joining NAB, I assumed that a big bank would be filled with bureaucratic people who were not necessarily forward thinkers. But it is not that way at all. In Australia, the big banks and consulting firms attract top talent and because of this, the bank is filled with smart, motivated people. Most people are well aware of the external threats of disruption. They are open to change, but making change happen at a large company can be challenging. The big Australian banks have shareholder bases that are interested in receiving a dividend, so it can be tough to make decisions for the long term that might mean sacrificing short-term cash flow.

How do you create an environment/culture that enables creativity and innovation?

NAB has made culture a priority with the creation of Labs and Ventures, and it has permeated throughout the bank by bringing start-ups with innovative thinking into the organization.

NAB Labs was set up to do proofs of concept based on the knowledge that many experiments are not going to work. The idea is to find the ones that do and then scale them. Most venture-backed companies will fail in that they do not return capital and/or go out of business. That is the nature of venture investing.

We have hackathons where anyone in the bank can present an idea, and the winner gets their idea turned into a proof of concept, which potentially transforms into a business or product. This is a great way to not only create new ideas but also identify entrepreneurial people.

Think about the last time you pitched (or have been pitched) an innovative idea. What worked well and what didn't?

There has to be a true passion. It helps if the founder is really passionate about the idea and has a good "story." Often, we see pitches that start by answering the question, "Why did I do this?" It is usually because of a personal experience. Because there are few original ideas we look more at the founders and whether we think they will be able to execute and succeed in a competitive environment.

I encourage entrepreneurs to tell the "team" story. Let prospective investors know who they are and why they are uniquely positioned to succeed. With less experienced entrepreneurs, I encourage them to fill the gaps by creating a strong advisory team. It gives comfort to prospective investors to see the founder is supported by others with relevant experience. It also demonstrates that the founder is capable of getting other people excited about their idea. Ultimately starting a company is about SELLING--selling to potential employees, customers, and investors.

Notes

1 For the latest news on venture capital and corporate venture capital in Australia, see www.avcal.com.au.
2 For archetypes of how corporates engage with start-ups and the effectiveness of the various approaches depending on the financial and strategic goals as well as organizational constraints, see Weiblen, T., & Chesbrough, H. W. (2015). Engaging with start-ups to enhance corporate innovation. *California Management Review, 57*(2), 66–90. In their study, they investigate many companies, including Siemens, AT&T, SAP, PayPal, and Bosch.
3 See https://www.nppa.com.au/.

PART III

Innovation: the future

CONCLUSION

Becoming a master of innovative ideas

This book began with a brief discussion of what innovation is, as well as how to become an innovator or inspire others in an innovative team. We discussed some of the myths around innovation. Some see technology as the road to innovation. A prevailing contemporary view is that doing anything even remotely associated with Artificial Intelligence or autonomous vehicles makes you an innovator. Others believe that taking an online course can make you a master of innovation. Our interviews, however, suggest otherwise. The wise words of the innovation experts interviewed for this book, coupled with the academic research highlighted, should guide you on your innovation journey and provide you with the effective ground rules that allow innovative ideas to flourish.

Reading about the stories, struggles, and successes of the innovators interviewed may be just the starting point on your road to innovation. But hopefully you have learned some invaluable lessons to guide you. First and foremost, the key to innovation is execution. Having ideas is not enough. Ideas abound and ideas are cheap. But making those ideas into something tangible – what we call execution – presents challenges. It is achievable, but it isn't always easy. Hopefully after reading this book you have learned about the skills needed to put ideas into practice.

Innovation is a never-ending journey, and the challenges that you encounter along the way are opportunities to learn. Start small and keep pushing the boundaries of your comfort zone (and those of others, too), whether these are domain expertise or the types of networks to which you have access. Engage with material from outside your field of expertise (buy a copy of *Monocle*, *Vogue*, *MIT Technology Review*, *Wired*, and *Domus*).[1] Attend meetings, exhibitions, and conferences outside your domain; over time your brain will start to rewire itself and create new patterns. Mingle with designers and architects.

Importantly, effective *mastering*, whether in innovation or elsewhere, will happen only when you reflect on what's happening around you and in your journey. Keeping a journal to capture your observations (and to jot down new ideas along the way) is a first step. The more you write things down, the more you will remember and create patterns over time. Your busy schedule means it's difficult to find the time to reflect, but you need to "make it a thing," a habit. Block time in your weekly schedule to reflect on learnings that have taken place. Make journaling the highlight of your day.[2] For your weekly reflection, close the door of your office, or book a meeting room for the same day and time each week, make sure you have a whiteboard and highlighters, and start making sense of where the world is heading and how things fit in, what has worked in your journey, and what needs to be improved. Return to the *6 Building Blocks for Innovation* to structure your reflections. Then you can match up your reflections to the different blocks in the framework. Over time, you might want to create your own interpretation of the framework or adapt parts of it.

We wrote *6 Building Blocks for Successful Innovation* to set you on a path toward excellence in innovation, whether it's coming up with innovative ideas, recognizing innovative ideas when they come to you, or leading teams that will develop innovations in your organization. Whether you are new at innovation or have done it before, having a lens through which to define innovation and look at the world around you is key. Our framework offers the guidance and discipline to give you confidence that you are on the right track and will be able to tackle the many challenges you will encounter along the way. You'll be able to find sources of inspiration, transform inspirations into ideas, and sell these ideas to the relevant stakeholders, whether they are colleagues you want to bring on the journey with you or those who have the power to say yes or no to your proposals. Being able to work effectively in the innovation area is immensely satisfying, not least because it gives you the power to inspire others who you meet along the way. As an innovator, you have the chance to make an impact in the world, small or large, just as we have seen in the journeys of the people featured in this book.

Notes

1 You might be less familiar with the last one unless you have been in the design and architecture space: here is the online version: https://www.domusweb.it/en.html.
2 Here we strongly suggest you read one of our favorite books on using time effectively, Knapp, J., & Zeratsky, J. (2018). *Make Time: How to Focus on What Matters Every Day.* New York: Currency. A wealth of tips and resources are available here: https://make-timebook.com/.

RESOURCES

This section of the book provides an overview of the frameworks referred to in the interviews. Some of them are classics, with which you might already be familiar. All of them will most certainly assist you in your innovation journey.

We also share some more recent approaches that we consider very effective, such as Design Sprints. The list below is not comprehensive and is intended as a starting point.

Alessi Formula for Success

Mentioned by: Carlo Gasparini

What is it about?

Alberto Alessi has developed a formula to test and predict the potential success of a new product in order to understand how the public may react if Alessi decides to produce it. The formula was originally developed in the early 1990s for making go/no-go decisions for prototypes moving into production. The formula consists of four parameters: (F) function, (P) price, (CL) communication potential, and (SMI) ability to stimulate sensation-memory-imaginary. For more details, refer to the interview with Carlo Gasparini.

When is it useful?

The Formula is useful for collecting feedback on a prototype or new product from both potential customers and internal experts. It can be very powerful when running interviews in person, as it allows people to elaborate their thoughts.

Complexity

The formula has been developed by Alessi for Alessi and as such can be highly specific to their strategy and vision. Depending on your business, you can use Alessi's formula as a starting point to develop your own and test it with potential customers.

Time required

There are two tasks. First, you need to determine your own formula and test it with potential customers. We recommend you take some time to do this and involve a wide range of people, including designers, artists, and so on to provide you with a fresh perspective on your business.

Second, once you have a prototype, interviews can be run with potential customers, but also employees and anyone who understands your business. This would require the usual time needed for interviews. If you follow the Sprint approach, you might not need many interviews, but you should develop a well-crafted system to collect and analyze feedback.

Resources

Alessi, A. (2016). *The Dream Factory: Alessi Since 1921*. Milan: Rizzoli.

Cynefin Framework

Mentioned by: Victoria Vallström (Bastide)

What is it about?

The Cynefin Framework provides guidance through decision making processes tailored for specific complex social situations. The framework, created by Dave Snowden in 1999 while working for IBM Global Services, is divided into four connecting quadrants that represent four decision making approaches, which can be used to manage situations of varying environmental complexity.

Quadrant 1: A simple situation exists when there are defined rules and a stable situation. The recommended approach is "sense, **categorize**, respond."

Quadrant 2: A complicated situation exists when the relationship between cause and effect is unclear, and analysis is necessary. The recommended approach is "sense, **analyze**, respond."

Quadrant 3: A complex situation exists when there are too many unknowns to analyze the situation, and any action can alter the situation. The leader should attempt to understand the situation before moving forward. The recommended approach is "**probe**, sense, respond."

Quadrant 4: A chaotic situation exists where adaption is necessary and is constantly changing. The leader should stabilize the situation before moving forward. The recommended approach is "**act**, sense, respond."

When is it useful?

This framework is useful anytime you need to make a decision. It can become part of your "decision making DNA."

Complexity

Medium. This is not the most straightforward framework, but it is incredibly useful to make sense of the environment in which your company operates.

Time required

We recommend spending two to three hours to digest and initially apply the framework, and then regularly revisit it to make sure you apply the principles to your cases at hand.

Resource

Snowden, D. J., & Boone, M. E. (2007). A leader's framework for decision making. *Harvard Business Review, 85*(11), 68.
https://www.youtube.com/watch?v=N7oz366X0-8.

Design-Driven Innovation

What is it about?

Design-driven innovation is an approach to innovation based on the observation that people do not just purchase products or services. They purchase "meaning" – where users' needs are not only satisfied by form and function, but also through experience (meaning).

Examples of meanings that a product or service might have for its users include the memories it invokes from childhood or travels, the extent and quality of interaction and enjoyment. Meaning is what makes a consumer identify with a product or service and how much the product or service becomes part of the person's identity.

A critical component of the process that leads to design-driven innovation is the engagement with "interpreters." Interpreters are individuals who understand and influence how people give meaning to things. Successful design-driven innovators are better than their competitors at identifying, attracting, and interacting with key interpreters. Design-driven innovation has the potential to create and change markets, enabling organizations to drive the market rather than simply adapt to it.

When is it useful?

Design-driven innovation is useful when your company is trying to identify new growth options in a radical way, for example brand-new products, product lines, or the complete reinvention of existing products.

Complexity

High. The success of the framework relies on engagement with so-called *interpreters* over a long period of time. The interpreters, along with long-term projects such as the ones performed by Alessi (e.g. Family Follows Fiction), take from a few weeks to a year or even longer and the engagement of a disparate set of interpreters, from artists, to architects, designers, sociologists and so on. However, these projects increase the likelihood of innovation of meanings and product lines that will be in production for a long period of time.

Alternatively, you can use one of the approaches that Alessi has taken (see Carlo Gasparini's interview as well as the **Alessi Formula for Success**) and invite anyone (even people from partly outside your industry) to make proposals. However, they have to know that you are open to even transgressive ideas and that you will implement some of these. If one of these two conditions is not satisfied, then you will end up with incremental innovation.

Time required

Depending on the depth and breadth of the project as well as how novel it is, we recommend to spend no less than a month but generally a longer time, for example up to a year or more.

Resources

Alessi, A. (2016). *The Dream Factory: Alessi Since 1921.* Milan: Rizzoli.
Verganti, R. (2009). *Design-Driven Innovation: Changing the Rules of Competition by Radically Innovating What Things Mean.* Boston, MA: Harvard Business Press.

Design Sprints

What is it about?

A design sprint is a five-day process for answering critical business questions through design, prototyping, and testing ideas with customers. Instead of waiting to launch a minimal product to understand if an idea is any good, you'll be able to achieve a good understanding from a realistic prototype.

The approach was originally developed at Google Ventures and is now used by numerous companies around the world. To find out more, refer to the book below which contains a wealth of tips on how to implement the process and make it successful.

Our experience in using Design Sprints: Don't take too many shortcuts from the framework because everything is there for a good reason. The process was tested and refined over a long period of time.

When is it useful?

As recommended in the book, Sprints are useful (1) when the stakes are high, and you are facing a big problem whose solution will require lots of money and time; (2) when you have a deadline and not enough time; or (3) you are stuck on a problem and lost momentum. Since running a sprint requires significant focused energy and expertise, use them only for big, important problems that your company is facing.

Complexity

Medium to high. The sprint runs for five full days plus some preparatory time (a couple of days) but requires focused attention from a group of senior people in your organization. A team of seven or fewer is about right, but you will also need to invite some experts for specific aspects of the sprint and then recruit potential customers to test the prototype. Thus, good planning is key to smooth execution.

Time required

Five full days plus preparatory time and some time afterward to follow up. There is a caveat here: When trying it for the first time, we recommend spending four weeks in total. The first week is needed to define the problem to solve and test it in advance with a few stakeholders, plus some background research. The second week serves to prepare the sprint itself. The third week is the actual sprint itself, and then there is some follow-up work to be done (including reflection on the outcome achieved) during the fourth week.

Resources

Knapp, J., Zeratsky, J., & Kowitz, B. (2016). *Sprint: How to Solve Big Problems and Test New Ideas in Just Five Days*. New York, NY: Simon & Schuster.
http://www.gv.com/sprint/

IDEO's sweet spot for innovation: desirability, viability, and feasibility

Mentioned by: Jeanne Marell

What is it about?

This framework was developed by IDEO to display the existence of innovation at the intersection of feasibility, desirability, and viability through a design-thinking approach. In order for innovation to eventually become successful, the idea must be feasible. That is, it should be potentially functional. It also must be desirable for consumers, so that they are willing to use the innovative product or process. Finally, innovative ideas must be viable, meaning that the idea is economically sustainable and will last well into the future. By analyzing the product under these three categories prior to development, innovators can fundamentally test their idea for long-term success and still have time to make necessary changes as gaps arise.

When is it useful?

The framework is fairly basic but can offer you a "back of the envelope" test of whether it is worth spending time to think further about a new idea. As such, it will come in handy anytime someone is presenting a new idea to you. Often, the idea might not be really useful for the final user (an idea looking for a problem, which is dangerous, as we tend to fall in love with our ideas) or it's not big enough to create viable streams of revenue for the business.

Complexity

Low. It should be part of the language of your organization anytime there is a new idea floating around.

Time required

Depending on the complexity of the idea being tested and how much research you need to do (whether primary research by talking to people or secondary research), this may take a few minutes or up to a couple of hours.

Resources

https://www.ideou.com/pages/design-thinking

The Double Diamond Framework (as part of Design Thinking)

Mentioned by: Jeanne Marell

What is it about?

The Double Diamond framework is a concept that is now part of the common language of designers and design-oriented business people alike. Fundamentally, it breaks down the creative process into four segments or phases.

The process begins with a problem. This is followed by the four segments, which are grouped in the two diamonds.

The segments are: discover, define, develop, and deliver.

The first diamond is made up of the "discover" and "define" segments. It comes into play when you are looking to understand the problem and the focus area. The first diamond is completed when a problem definition and design brief are formed.

The second diamond consists of the "develop" and "deliver" segments, where potential solutions are first sketched and iteratively tested. The delivery section is concluded when a solution is reached.

Both diamonds are necessary parts of the framework to ensure that the problem is fully understood before a complete and accurate solution is developed. The diamond reminds you when to use divergent thinking and when to use convergent thinking. During the divergent thinking phases, you generate the greatest number of possible ideas, fundamentally withholding judgment. In the convergent phase you narrow down the ideas into a manageable set.

Importantly, the Double Diamond suggests that this happens twice: you first diverge when you define the problem, then you converge into one problem definition, then you diverge in the generation of possible solutions before you converge into one solution. The common problem encountered is that there is not long enough divergent phases or the first diamond is skipped altogether.

When is it useful?

All the time! It's something to keep in mind any time you are involved in an innovative project, whether you need to generate, evaluate, prototype, or implement ideas. Knowing which phase you are in allows you to switch your brain from convergent to divergent thinking and non-judgment to judgment, respectively.

Complexity

Medium. The concept itself is easily understood. It is more difficult to put it into practice on a daily basis.

Time required

You may need an hour or two to understand the framework and do regular reviews to make sure you don't forget the key principles.

Resource

https://www.designcouncil.org.uk/news-opinion/design-process-what-double-diamond

Journey Mapping (aka experience mapping; as part of Design Thinking)

Mentioned by: Stefan Vlachos

What is it about?

Journey mapping, together with persona profiling, is a powerful method of under-standing what customers do, think, and feel during an experience, whether it's purchasing, using, or disposing of a product or service. By presenting a visual rep-resentation of the complete user experience, journey maps allow viewers to under-stand consumer needs and satisfaction levels. Together with the Double Diamond, this is a well-known tool in design thinking, which usually takes place at the start of the innovation journey to better understand user needs.

To really take advantage of this framework, we recommend using it in conjunction with ethnographic approaches that look deeply into the effects of culture on consumers. Grant McCracken has investigated the role of culture in relation to collaboration, problem solving, and innovation (see McCracken, 2011). If you want to learn more about using ethnography to run interviews, see McCracken (1988). Additional excellent resources for journey mapping or experience mapping are Liedtka and Ogilvie (2011) and Fraser (2012).

When is it useful?

Journey mapping is useful when you have an existing product or service and you are looking at new ways to improve it. It is less applicable when you are thinking about creating brand-new products and services.

Complexity

Medium to high (if you want to do it well). To get the most from the activity, you need anthropologists and designers on board, as they have a different approach to observing humans and their activities. Their years of training allow them to look at the situation without judgment and really see through the eyes of the users. Employing a business person with one day of training in design thinking is not going allow you the depth you need (we have seen it done over and over again). Typically, all you get are observations colored with the glasses of feasibility (that is, business people tend to be biased in favor of the status quo and against breaking the rules of what's possible and feasible).

Time required

For each journey you need to set up the study (type of people to interview, recruit participants), run the observations and interviews, and then make sense of the data. A few weeks to a few months are needed.

Resources

Fraser, H. M. (2012). *Design Works: How to Tackle Your Toughest Innovation Challenges Through Business Design*. Toronto: University of Toronto Press.

Liedtka, J., & Ogilvie, T. (2011). *Designing for Growth: A Design Thinking Toolkit for Managers*. New York, NY: Columbia University Press.

McCracken, G. D. (1988). *The Long Interview* (Vol. 13). Newbury Park, CA: Sage.

McCracken, G. D. (2011). *Chief Culture Officer: How to Create a Living, Breathing Corporation*: Basic Books.

Corporate Engagement Models with start-ups/or start-up engagement strategy

What is it about?

The Corporate Engagement Model summarizes strategies that are available to executives who seek to tap into entrepreneurial innovation, whether it is generated within the corporation or outside. The article, where the model was developed, also provides a wealth of examples on how other companies do it in practice. Both Peter Löfgren, and Melissa Widner have discussed their approaches to some extent and below we expand somewhat and provide you with some guidelines about the possibilities.

The model highlights four types of lightweight models to engage with start-ups in an attempt to accelerate decision making and the ability to attract and retain start-ups, even in large quantities.

The model asks two fundamental questions: First, what is the goal a company wants to achieve through engagement with start-ups? For example, are you aiming to insource entrepreneurial creativity from the outside (outside-in innovation), or do you want to utilize start-up agility to push your own innovations to the market (inside-out innovation). Second, do you want to gain insights or to control and participate in the upside with an equity stake? In other terms, are you looking for strategic or financial benefits?

The combination of these two dimensions (direction of the flow of innovation and equity participation) determines the forms of engagement and success factors. The original model discusses corporate venturing, corporate incubation, and start-up programs, including platforms, for engaging with start-ups.

When is it useful?

The model can be particularly useful to develop your company's sensing capabilities.

Complexity

Medium. This framework can help you map the options you have available and have a conversation within your company on what is the most suitable way forward given your resources and desired time frame. We recommend complementing it with resources such as CB Insights, Crunchbase, and Angel.co to scout for start-ups across the world.

Time required

It really depends on the goal (strategic or financial). But it ultimately comes down to the effort needed to select and engage with start-ups. The analysis of the start-up space will be continuous.

Resources

Weiblen, T., & Chesbrough, H. W. (2015). Engaging with start-ups to enhance corporate innovation. *California Management Review, 57*(2), 66–90.

Three Horizon Model

Mentioned by: Mark Nierwetberg, and Stefan Vlachos

What is it about?

The Three Horizon Model was established to provide guidance for companies in relation to innovation and growth by defining three key focus areas when making investment decisions.

Horizon 1: Companies should focus on making improvements to their current business to increase profits and reach their greatest potential within the existing structure.

Horizon 2: Companies should pursue entrepreneurial opportunities despite the risk of investment to expand beyond the existing structure and bring in additional profits in the future.

Horizon 3: Companies should search for long-term opportunities to enter new businesses that may not currently be profitable but will eventually sustain a profitable and growing company in the future.

When is it useful?

All the time. This is one of the frameworks you should have in mind when designing an organization's business units and setting goals and KPIs, as well as hiring people.

Complexity

Low. The difficulty is in realizing the three different parts of the framework at the same time.

Time required

You will need about a month for research and setup and then another week each year to make sure everything is on track.

Resources

Baghai, M., Coley, S., & White, D. (2000). *The Alchemy of Growth*. Reading, MA: Basic Books.

Harreld, J. B., O'Reilly III, C. A., & Tushman, M. L. (2007). Dynamic capabilities at IBM: Driving strategy into action. *California Management Review, 49*(4), 21–43.

Nagji, B., & Tuff, G. (2012). Managing your innovation portfolio. *Harvard Business Review*, 66–73.

QUESTION INDEX

In this section, we include the questions that we used in our interviews. All respondents answered the first question about innovative ideas and then they were allowed to pick those about which they felt most passionate. Below you'll find the list of questions as well as the respondents who addressed each question. Note that a few respondents were asked also additional questions to allow them to expand on their thoughts. These are not included in the list below.

1. **Let's first talk about "innovative ideas". Can you give us examples, including personal experiences, if you like? They can be new ways about approaching problems, new ways of doing things, new products or services, new experiences and the way the user interacts with products, new business models, establishing entirely new teams and businesses.**
   Carlo Gasparini, 44; Céline Le Cotonnec, 51; Peter Löfgren, 60; Jeanne Marell, 66; Christine Ng, 74; Mark Nierwetberg, 81; Tim Romero, 89; Stephen Simpson, 95; Paul Slezak, 103; André Teixeira, 110; Cindy Tripp, 121; Victoria Vallström (Bastide), 133; Stefan Vlachos, 142; Melissa Widner, 150.

2. **What is the one thing that you do regularly (e.g., daily, quarterly, annually) which has contributed to your success spotting innovative ideas/solutions?**
   Céline Le Cotonnec, 54; Christine Ng, 76; Tim Romero, 89; André Teixeira, 111

3. **Where do you find sources of inspiration for new ideas or opportunities?**
   Carlo Gasparini, 46; Jeanne Marell, 70; Tim Romero, 90; Paul Slezak, 104; André Teixeira, 112; Stefan Vlachos, 144; Melissa Widner, 151.

ABOUT THE RESEARCH

In case you are curious about how we came up with the original book idea and the research behind it, here is the full story.

As you probably know by now, Massimo is primarily an academic and consultant, while Moritz is a consultant, entrepreneur, and author. We talked about writing together for a long time given that we have worked together on multiple projects. Companies kept asking us, "What is everyone else doing in terms of innovation? How did they start their journey? What can we learn from them so we don't make obvious mistakes?"

Academic studies have lots to say but haven't caught up yet with much of what is going on in the real world. Disruption from some clever start-ups is shaking up industries such as banking, insurance, healthcare, but also retail, real estate, and much more. Innovation is no longer an option, it's a must. And companies that haven't yet started on the road to innovation need to catch up very quickly while avoiding the mistakes of the early "adopters."

Over the 2017–2018 holiday break we had a lightbulb moment. One of us went to visit Zappos and learned firsthand about its amazing way of doing things. At the same time, we read *Tribe of Mentors* by Tim Ferris, a book based on interviews with exceptional individuals. The lightbulb was switched on: what if we interviewed the people from around the world who had done great things in the innovation space? The well known and the lesser known? That's how the book started.

So, we created a list of questions and then applied some recommendations from the Design Sprint approach[1] to refine it until we drilled down to a list of 15 questions that, based on our experience, we knew people wanted an answer to but that people also wanted to share their perspective on. We also identified our persona, our target audience, those who would most benefit from the book, on the basis of our continuous interactions with managers and executives.

In the spirit of design thinking, we both thought about the people to interview and developed the questions for testing. We selected five individuals (according to Jake Knapp and John Zeratsky and their Design Sprint book, five subjects will identify 85% of the problems of a new concept). We made it to four – thanks to Josh Mahaney from Orlando Magic, John Corleto from Future Brands, Carlos Vazquez, PhD student at the University of Sydney Business School and ex-Global Innovation Delivery Manager at Pernot Ricard Winemakers, and Paul Slezak, CEO of RecruitLoop, who was so passionate about the project and who also is an interviewee in the book.

We then sent out an invitation to be interviewed to many of the people we have admired for a long time, and we received overwhelmingly enthusiastic feedback.

The interviews took place over the course of the year, and then the interview transcripts were polished and in some cases, further discussion was conducted with the respondents. We then analyzed the interviews using NVivo,[2] a software commonly used for qualitative research. With our academic hats on, we extrapolated a series of themes and identified many commonalities among the interviews. This allowed us to understand the key points of innovation on a deeper level from a range of unique points of view. The high-level themes we established were represented by ten keywords or points that repeatedly appeared throughout the interviews. By establishing ten categories, we were able to conduct additional coding within NVivo to further analyze and compare the interviews in a simplified yet meaningful way. A "code," in technical terms, is a word or short phrase that assigns a "summative, salient, essence-capturing, and/or evocative attribute" for a portion of language.

After completing the extensive coding process and assigning specific words and phrases to each interview, we discussed these key themes together with a team of research assistants and then tested these themes with two people outside the research to grasp their understanding of our work (Did it make sense to them too? Are we missing anything)? These key themes became a focus piece for the other sections of our book.

Then we started writing. After the first draft of the entire manuscript, we engaged with several test readers from a variety of backgrounds, from design thinking and innovation, to consulting, engineering, psychology, and media. After a few iterations, here is our book! We hope it takes you on an empowering innovation journey guided by the curated wisdom of those who have made innovation happen in their companies.

Notes

1 Knapp, J., Zeratsky, J., & Kowitz, B. (2016). *Sprint: How to Solve Big Problems and Test New Ideas in Just Five Days.* New York, NY: Simon and Schuster.
2 If you are interested in the process of coding of qualitative research, see Saldaña, J. (2015). *The Coding Manual for Qualitative Researchers.* London, UK: Sage.

INDEX

List of Companies and Organizations Mentioned